PABLO PICASSO

by Stuart A. Kallen

LUCENT BOOKS
A part of Gale, Cengage Learning

GALE
CENGAGE Learning™

Detroit • New York • San Francisco • New Haven, Conn • Waterville, Maine • London

GALE
CENGAGE Learning

LIBRARY OF CONGRESS CATALOGING-IN-PUBLICATION DATA

Kallen, Stuart A., 1955–
   Pablo Picasso / by Stuart A. Kallen.
      p. cm. — (Eye on art)
   Includes bibliographical references and index.
   ISBN 978-1-4205-0045-5 (hardcover)
   1. Picasso, Pablo, 1881–1973—Juvenile literature. 2. Artists—France—Biography—Juvenile literature. I. Title.
   N6853.P5K35 2009
   709'.2—dc22
   [B]
                                        2008013338

Lucent Books
27500 Drake Rd
Farmington Hills MI 48331

ISBN-13: 978-1-4205-0045-5
ISBN-10: 1-4205-0045-7

Printed in the United States of America
1 2 3 4 5 6 7 13 12 11 10 09

CONTENTS

Foreword

"Art has no other purpose than to brush aside . . . everything that veils reality from us in order to bring us face to face with reality itself."

—French philosopher Henri-Louis Bergson

Some thirty-one thousand years ago, early humans painted strikingly sophisticated images of horses, bison, rhinoceroses, bears, and other animals on the walls of a cave in southern France. The meaning of these elaborate pictures is unknown, although some experts speculate that they held ceremonial significance. Regardless of their intended purpose, the Chauvet-Pont-d'Arc cave paintings represent some of the first known expressions of the artistic impulse.

From the Paleolithic era to the present day, human beings have continued to create works of visual art. Artists have developed painting, drawing, sculpture, engraving, and many other techniques to produce visual representations of landscapes, the human form, religious and historical events, and countless other subjects. The artistic impulse also finds expression in glass, jewelry, and new forms inspired by new technology. Indeed, judging by humanity's prolific artistic output throughout history, one must conclude that the compulsion to produce art is an inherent aspect of being human, and the results are among humanity's greatest cultural achievements: masterpieces such as the architectural marvels of ancient Greece, Michelangelo's perfectly rendered statue *David*, Vincent van Gogh's visionary painting *Starry Night*, and endless other treasures.

The creative impulse serves many purposes for society. At its most basic level, art is a form of entertainment or the means for a satisfying or pleasant aesthetic experience. But art's true power lies not in its potential to entertain and delight but in its ability to enlighten, to reveal the truth, and by doing so to uplift the human spirit and transform the human race.

One of the primary functions of art has been to serve religion. For most of Western history, for example, artists were paid by the church to produce works with religious themes and subjects. Art was thus a tool to help human beings transcend mundane, secular reality and achieve spiritual enlightenment. One of the best-known, and largest-scale, examples of Christian religious art is the Sistine Chapel in the Vatican in Rome. In 1508 Pope Julius II commissioned Italian Renaissance artist Michelangelo to paint the chapel's vaulted ceiling, an area of 640 square yards (535 sq. m). Michelangelo spent four years on scaffolding, his neck craned, creating a panoramic fresco of some three hundred human figures. His paintings depict Old Testament prophets and heroes, sibyls of Greek mythology, and nine scenes from the Book of Genesis, including the Creation of Adam, the Fall of Adam and Eve from the Garden of Eden, and the Flood. The ceiling of the Sistine Chapel is considered one of the greatest works of Western art and has inspired the awe of countless Christian pilgrims and other religious seekers. As eighteenth-century German poet and author Johann Wolfgang von Goethe wrote, "Until you have seen this Sistine Chapel, you can have no adequate conception of what man is capable of."

In addition to inspiring religious fervor, art can serve as a force for social change. Artists are among the visionaries of any culture. As such, they often perceive injustice and wrongdoing and confront others by reflecting what they see in their work. One classic example of art as social commentary was created in May 1937, during the brutal Spanish civil war. On May 1 Spanish artist Pablo Picasso learned of the recent attack on the small Basque village of Guernica by German airplanes allied with fascist forces led by Francisco Franco. The German pilots had used the village for target practice, a three-hour bombing that killed sixteen hundred civilians. Picasso, living in Paris, channeled his outrage over the massacre into his painting *Guernica,* a black, white, and gray mural that depicts dismembered animals and fractured human figures whose faces are contorted in agonized expressions. Initially, critics and the public condemned the painting as an incoherent hodgepodge, but the work soon came to be seen as a powerful antiwar statement and remains an iconic symbol of the violence and terror that dominated world events during the remainder of the twentieth century.

The impulse to create art—whether painting animals with crude pigments on a cave wall, sculpting a human form from marble, or commemorating human tragedy in a mural—thus serves many purposes. It offers an entertaining diversion, nourishes the imagination and the spirit, decorates and beautifies the world, and chronicles the age. But underlying all these functions is the desire to reveal that which is obscure—to illuminate, clarify, and perhaps ennoble. As Picasso himself stated, "The purpose of art is washing the dust of daily life off our souls."

The Eye on Art series is intended to assist readers in understanding the various roles of art in society. Each volume offers an in-depth exploration of a major artistic movement, medium, figure, or profession. All books in the series are beautifully illustrated with full-color photographs and diagrams. Riveting narrative, clear technical explanation, informative sidebars, fully documented quotes, a bibliography, and a thorough index all provide excellent starting points for research and discussion. With these features, the Eye on Art series is a useful introduction to the world of art—a world that can offer both insight and inspiration.

Introduction

A Creative Force of Nature

Only a few times in history has a single creative person produced work that changed not only the world of art but the very way the public perceives the world. Such an individual was Spanish artist Pablo Picasso. Small, muscular, with radiant black eyes, Picasso was a master at drawing, painting, sculpting, graphics, ceramics, and theatrical design. His career spanned nearly the entire era of modern art, starting with the realism era in the late nineteenth century and drawing to a close with the advent of neo-Expressionism, a style inspired by Picasso's last works. During the intervening years, Picasso was a virtuoso in a variety of styles including expressionism, cubism, and surrealism, styles that define twentieth-century art. And at every juncture Picasso broke the established rules to create new artistic realties that used symbolism, abstraction, and distorted imagery to express visions about war, peace, love, happiness, and heartbreak.

Picasso's works have been described as surprising, extraordinary, emotional, compelling, original, and sensuous. Like many creative geniuses, however, his life was wrapped in contradictions. His paintings brought joy to millions of viewers but were created by a man who often suffered deep despair from both personal problems and the European wars that raged around him. The painter joined the Communist Party hoping to create a more equal society, while at the same time he was an egotistical millionaire who jealously guarded his privacy to the point of shutting out those who loved him most. Referring to Picasso's personal life, his granddaughter Marina Picasso writes, "He drove everyone who got near him to despair,"[1] and his second wife, mistress, and grandson all committed suicide. Perhaps this is because Picasso could not separate himself from his art, declaring, "The more you put yourself into it . . . the closer you get to the truth."[2]

Those who did not have to deal with the artist's demons may be thankful for the personal sacrifices he made for art.

Picasso stands in his studio amid various pieces of his work. He is considered both the most prolific artist ever and the most influential artist of the twentieth century.

During the seventy-five years of his professional career, Picasso produced around 13,500 paintings, 100,000 prints and engravings, 34,000 book illustrations, and 300 sculptures, securing his place in the *Guinness Book of World Records* as the most prolific artist ever. This huge body of matchless creativity is noted not just for its quantity but its astounding quality, and Picasso's vision permanently changed the direction of modern art. As *Time* magazine art critic Robert Hughes concludes:

> To say that Pablo Picasso dominated Western art in the 20th century is, by now, the merest commonplace. Before his 50th birthday, the little Spaniard from Málaga had become the very prototype of the modern artist as public figure. No painter before him had had a mass audience in his own lifetime. . . . There was scarcely a 20th century movement that he didn't inspire, contribute to or—in the case of Cubism—beget. Quite simply, as well as being a force of culture, Picasso was also a force of nature.[3]

A Young Artist

Picasso's life was unusual from the very moment of his birth in the sunny town of Málaga on the southern coast of Spain. When the first child of José Ruiz Blasco and Maria Picasso de Ruiz was born at 11:15 P.M. on October 25, 1881, the baby was not breathing and was presumed dead. After a few minutes, however, Pablo's uncle, Salvador Ruiz, leaned into the baby's face and blew a stream of cigar smoke up his nose. Within seconds, the baby began to scream and, as Norman Mailer writes in *Portrait of Picasso as a Young Man*, "A genius was born. His first breath . . . entered on a rush of smoke, searing to the throat, scorching his lungs, and laced with the stimulants of nicotine."[4]

Two weeks later the baby was baptized Pablo Diego José Francisco de Paula Juan Nepomuceno María de los Remedios Cipriano de la Santísima Trinidad, a string of names meant to honor grandparents, relatives, and saints. At the end of this unusually long moniker, two more names were attached, Ruiz y Picasso, representing his father's and mother's families respectively, as is the Spanish tradition. During his early years as an artist, Pablo did not sign his entire name, which would have required a very large canvas, but used the names P. Ruiz or P.

Ruiz Picasso. In 1902 he dropped the Ruiz and was thereafter known as P. Picasso.

That Pablo became an artist was no surprise to those who knew his family. José, nicknamed "the Englishman" for his a tall stature, blue eyes, reddish hair, and fondness for English ways, was an artist and an art teacher. José also raised pigeons and often used them for subjects in his work. Picasso later stated that his father's paintings were "dining room pictures, the kind with partridges and pigeons, hares and rabbits, fur and feathers."[5] In addition, José was employed as a curator, or head administrator, at the Metropolitan Museum of Málaga where he oversaw the collection and restored paintings. Other members of Pablo's family, such as his uncles, aunts, and grandparents, were either artists or devoted art patrons. Little wonder then that Pablo's first word was *piz,* baby talk for *lápiz,* or pencil, in Spanish.

A Different Way of Seeing

Even before he learned his first words, Pablo was recognized as a child prodigy. The pictures he drew were not the typical scrawls of a two-year-old but complex spirals that covered entire sheets of paper. Maria described these designs as *torruellas,* a word for churros or pastries, and these elaborate coils would be seen in Picasso's work throughout his lifetime. For example, the coiled braids in Picasso's 1903 painting *Woman in Blue with a Beret* recall the spirals that his mother said he drew before he could speak.

José quickly recognized his son's genius and began giving him art lessons. By the time he was seven, Pablo was drawing his father's pigeons as well as horses, burros, and other animals that could be found in the streets of Málaga. At the age of eleven, Pablo had developed skills to the point where he could sketch the realistic likeness of an entire animal in a continuous single line. He was also able to skillfully cut the images from paper and make puppets that he used to project shadows on the wall with a candle-powered lantern.

Even as he developed his artistic talents, Pablo was miserable as a student. Rebellious in nature, he hated following rules, and when not cutting classes he spent his time at his desk drawing pictures and ignoring his teachers. Hoping to improve his attitude, Pablo's parents enrolled him in the best private school in Málaga. However, he feared the other boys at school and often threw temper tantrums or feigned illness to avoid attending school.

As a result of his refusal to pay attention in school, Picasso later claimed he never learned the proper sequence of the alphabet. He was just as hopeless with math because numbers, rather than being mathematical concepts, seemed to him to represent shapes and forms. For example, the number 7 looked like an upside-down nose while 4 might look like a sailboat. Reflecting on a math test he failed at the age of seven, Picasso later told close friend and biographer Jaime Sabartés that instead of seeing a math problem, he associated the numbers with his favorite art topic: "The little eye of the pigeon is round like a 0. Under the 0 is a 6 for the breast, underneath that a 3. The eyes are like 2's, and so are the wings."[6]

"Excellent with Honorable Mention"

Pablo's problems at school were largely ignored by his parents because the boy's talents were becoming more obvious every day. When he was only eight years old, he created his first oil painting. It was not a childish drawing but a depiction of a picador, or bullfighter, on horseback. This painting was doubtlessly inspired by the many bullfights the boy had attended with his father, who was an enthusiastic fan of the sport. Pablo too would become a passionate patron of the bullring, and bullfighting would remain a constant source of inspiration for his paintings.

In 1890 the Metropolitan Museum of Málaga closed its doors, leaving José without a job to support his family which now included Pablo and his two younger sisters, Lola and Concepción, nicknamed Conchita. Several months later José was offered a job as a drawing teacher at the Da Guarda Institute in Corunna, a town on the Atlantic coast seven hundred miles north of Málaga.

Picasso's first oil painting, *The Little Picador,* was created when the artist was eight years old.

In October 1891, shortly before his tenth birthday, Pablo moved to Corunna where he began his formal art education at the School of Fine Art. Unlike previous years, when he had to be dragged to school by the family maid, Picasso thrived in the academic atmosphere of the art school. With amazing powers of observation and skill, the young artist eagerly performed his lessons, copying oil paintings made by masters, sketching Greek and Roman sculptures, and making charcoal drawings of live models. Teachers praised the work, and Picasso's grades ranged from "Excellent" to "Excellent with honorable mention." However, this rigorous form of schooling left little room for creativity, as Lael Wertenbaker explains in *The World of Picasso*: "The aim was to produce exact likenesses, and the student who could not do so was believed to have no future as a painter. Such an approach left little room for imagination or originality."[7]

Pablo enthusiastically tapped his creative powers when he was not attending school. By the time he was thirteen, the diminutive boy with the sketchbooks tucked under his arm had become a fixture on the beaches and streets of Corunna. As he watched people making their way down the street in the stormy weather that was common to the town, Pablo drew quick, accurate sketches. Underneath he inserted humorous captions such as "The rain has begun and will continue until summer. . . . Also the wind has begun and will continue until Corunna is no more."[8]

In addition to street sketches, Pablo was fond of drawing self-portraits and creating lifelike paintings of his sisters and parents. However, while the young man seemed to be thriving in Corunna, his father was unhappy at work and was lonely for his family and friends in sunny Málaga where he had lived his entire life. Oftentimes he would come home from work and stare listlessly out the window at the rain.

The damp weather of Corunna was a breeding ground for disease as well as depression. In late 1894 seven-year-old Conchita fell ill with diphtheria, a highly contagious disease of the respiratory system. Pablo was stunned by this turn of events and made a promise to God that if his sister's life was spared, he would give up the thing he loved most, painting. Sixty years later, Picasso spoke about this vow for the first time, saying that it was ignored by God, and when Conchita died on January 10, 1895, he was

As a young art student, Picasso enjoyed creating self-portraits such as this one, which he painted when he was around fifteen years old.

wracked with guilt, feeling that his talents were now a result of his sister's death. These feelings were compounded a few weeks later when José gave up painting and turned his paint and canvases over to his son. Wertenbaker describes the situation:

> One evening Don José returned from a stroll to find that Pablo had taken one of his unfinished sketches—of a pigeon—and painted with exquisite precision the talons and the delicate feathering along the bird's legs. The effect was better than anything the father himself had ever achieved. Ambivalently gripped with pride and despair, Don José handed his own palette and brushes to his son, then 13, and vowed never to paint again.[9]

Rebellion in Barcelona

Pablo's family suffered through another year in Corunna before José found a teaching job at the School of Fine Arts in Barcelona. Before the family moved, in February 1895, José set up an exhibition of his son's paintings in a small storefront in Corunna's fashionable shopping district. Pablo's works included oil paintings such as *Portrait of a Bearded Man*, *Portrait of Don José*, *Beggar in a Cap*, and *Girl with Bare Feet*. Although these paintings clearly display the talents of a competent artist, few were sold when word leaked out that the artist was only thirteen. However, a local reviewer writes, "if he continues in the courageous and mature manner, there is no doubt that he has days of glory and a brilliant future ahead of him."[10]

Such reviews bolstered Pablo's already large ego and encouraged his rebellious spirit. This was seen several months later when he took his entrance exams for the Barcelona School of Fine Arts, called La Llotja. Instructed to produce two precise and realistic drawings of a male model, Pablo, according to Arianna Huffington in her book *Picasso: Creator and Destroyer*, drew the model "once naked and looking bad-tempered, and once looking even more ridiculous wrapped in a sheet. . . . The feet were left unfinished, as though he could not be bothered with such details for a mere admissions test."[11] Picasso

His Guilt Was Enormous

Picasso was known as a lifelong atheist, and some have theorized that the artist began questioning his beliefs at the age of thirteen when his sister died. In Picasso: Creator and Destroyer, *Arianna Huffington describes the complex emotions felt by the artist upon Conchita's death:*

On January 10, [1895] his eight-year-old sister, Conchita, died of diphtheria. Pablo watched her deteriorate from the smiling little girl with the blond curls whom he had so tenderly drawn to the ghost of herself that he drew just before death snatched her away. . . . In his anguish, Pablo made a terrible pact with God. He offered to sacrifice his gift to Him and never pick up a brush again if He would save Conchita. And then he was torn between wanting her saved and wanting her dead so that his gift would be saved. When she died, he decided that God was evil and destiny an enemy. At the same time he was convinced that it was his ambivalence that had made it possible for God to kill Conchita. His guilt was enormous . . . [and] it was compounded by his primitive, almost magical, conviction that his little sister's death had released him to be a painter and follow the call of the power he had been given, whatever the consequences.

Arianna Huffington, *Picasso: Creator and Destroyer.* New York: Simon & Schuster, 1988, p. 30.

later bragged that he had been given one month to produce the two pictures but finished them both in one day. Research shows, however, it took the young artist five days to produce the pictures that won him a place in the prestigious art school without accurately completing the assignment.

Not yet fourteen, Pablo was several years younger than most of the other students at La Llotja. However, he was already feeling that school had little more to offer him. He deeply resented the demands of his teachers, thought their lessons were mediocre, and was openly proud that he could barely read or write. In short, Pablo was becoming a young rebel, rejecting the conventions and traditions of school, and by extension, society at large. And, as Huffington writes, "It was an attitude which fitted perfectly with the mood of rebellion and anarchy that pervaded Barcelona at the time. . . . Barcelona was the anarchist capital of Europe."[12]

Young Picasso, pictured here around the age of 18, had a passion for creating art for as long as he could remember. He had very little interest in the traditional subjects taught in school.

The anarchy was a reaction to widespread corruption that revolutionaries saw in government and religious institutions. Violence was the tool of the anarchists, and the 1890s are remembered in Barcelona as a decade of terrorism and harsh retaliation by authorities. In 1893 a young anarchist threw two bombs at a military procession, killing several politicians and soldiers. A few months later a revolutionary tossed several bombs into the orchestra pit at the opera house, killing twenty-two. As a wave of attacks continued, authorities arrested and tortured thousands of young men, many of them innocent of any crime except sympathizing with the anarchists. Dozens were publicly executed.

Many artists, writers, and intellectuals, including Pablo, supported the anarchists. According to Mailer:

> The art students he met at La Llotja, as seen through the eyes of [the young painter], were anarchists, madmen, wild men—in short, young middle class students like himself. Still, they could feel themselves possessed of a genuine mission. Surrounded by a stifling bourgeois world that was virtually summoning them to throw it over, they were full of intoxication that yes, they were the ones who would do it. . . . [Picasso] would live in [Barcelona] for the next five years [and] it proved to be a powerful, fearful, stimulating adolescence.[13]

Major Recognition

Whatever the political climate, Pablo still lived at home with his parents, and José continued to play an important role in the boy's life. In 1896 Pablo's father convinced his son to create a painting to commemorate Lola's first communion. The resulting work, *First Communion*, is hardly revolutionary, a painting in the typical realistic style of the time depicting a father, daughter, and altar boy performing a communion ceremony.

First Communion received little attention when it was shown at the Exhibition of Fine Arts in Barcelona. However,

Pablo's next major work, *Science and Charity*, brought the young painter his first major recognition. *Science and Charity* portrays a bedside scene where a doctor, again modeled by José, tends to an ailing woman while a nun looks on, holding the sick woman's child in her arms. This picture, the first painted in a little studio José rented for his son, received honorable mention at the national fine arts exhibition in Madrid and won a gold medal at the Málaga Provincial Exhibition. In celebration of this achievement, renowned Málaga painter Martínez de la Vega grandly baptized Pablo as a successful artist, pouring champagne over his head at the reception.

In Málaga, José and Pablo's uncle Salvador decided that the young painter had a bright future as an academic artist and took up a collection among family members to send him to the Royal Academy of San Fernando in Madrid. This prestigious school was the best in Spain and required Pablo's relatives to donate considerable funds for tuition and living expenses. According to Marilyn McCully in *Picasso: The Early Years, 1892–1906*, Picasso later recalled that "family members pooled their financial sources to send him to Madrid as if they were buying shares in his future."[14]

Despite the financial commitment, Pablo quickly lost interest in his lessons at the Royal Academy, skipping classes to sit in cafés, parks, and on street corners making sketches. This angered his aunts and uncles, who then stopped sending Pablo money. Soon the artist was unable to afford a studio and was reduced to living in an unheated room where he came down with scarlet fever. Not able to take care of himself, Pablo returned to Barcelona, his face gaunt, his body emaciated.

A New Use of Color and Freedom of Line

While Pablo had been largely friendless in Madrid, when he returned home in 1898 he was able to reunite with his best friend, Manuel Pallarés, who had worked beside him in his anatomy class at Llotja. Pallarés was five years older than Pablo, but the two spent a great deal of time together, drinking in cafés and patronizing the brothels in Barcelona's notorious Chinatown neighborhood. Commenting on their relationship many years later, Pallarés recalled Picasso "neither seemed nor acted like a boy his age. He was very mature."[15]

After a short stay with his family in Barcelona, Pablo moved to the Pallarés family home in the isolated mountain village of Horta de Sant Joan. For the next eight months the boy from the city learned about life in the countryside. He chopped wood, cooked simple meals over a campfire, and showered under a waterfall. Many weeks were spent wandering

HE GRASPED EVERYTHING VERY QUICKLY

Picasso began a lifelong friendship with painter Manuel Pallarés in the mid-1890s when attending art school in Barcelona. In 1972, at the age of ninety-six, Pallarés recalled Picasso the teenager:

He had a very strong personality, appealing, and way ahead of the others who were all five or six years older. He grasped everything very quickly; paid no apparent attention to what the professors were saying. Picasso . . . had an extraordinary curiosity . . . took things in the blink of an eye, and remembered them months later. In everything he was different. . . . Sometimes very excited, at other times he could go for hours without saying a word. . . . He could get angry quickly but calm down just as fast. He was aware of his superiority over us, but never showed it. He often seemed melancholy as if he had just thought of some sad things. His face would cloud over, his eyes become dark.

Quoted in Norman Mailer, *Portrait of Picasso as a Young Man.* New York: Atlantic Monthly, 1995, p. 16.

THOUSANDS OF WRETCHES

When Picasso returned to Barcelona after eight months painting in the mountains, he found the city full of wounded soldiers living in poverty. Spain had just lost Cuba and the Philippines to the United States in the Spanish-American War, and revolution was in the air. Art scholar Pierre Cabanne describes the city as Picasso saw it in Pablo Picasso: His Life and Times:

*A*longside its anarchist troublemakers and . . . its staid bourgeois and pious industrialists, it had a horribly poverty-stricken population, living in sordid filth; thousands of wretches were penned into the notorious *barrio chino* [Chinatown] where a dubious fauna of whores, killers, deserters, [robbers] and street urchins permeated the huge mass of workers exploited by their bosses. . . . [Now] there were super-added the sick and wounded [soldiers] repatriated from forever-lost Cuba, forgotten and made to order for the fomenters of rebellion.

Pierre Cabanne, *Pablo Picasso: His Life and Times.* New York: William Morrow, 1977, p. 46.

the region's fertile valleys and mountain trails with Pallarés, paint boxes, canvases, easels, and camping gear strapped to the backs of mules. According to the Web site of the Museu Picasso, or Picasso Museum, in Barcelona, the paintings of the countryside and its inhabitants created during this period are

a point of reference in his artistic development because of their frank, spontaneous and luminous character. The paintings show a new use of color and a great freedom of line, brushstroke and luminosity. [This period] marked his first serious step towards distancing himself from academic art, and he made a firm decision to search for new forms of artistic expression. At Horta de Sant Joan . . . his formal rupture with the official art world became a firm stance.[16]

Perhaps this is why Picasso later declared, "Whatever I know, I learned in Horta."[17]

Although he was not yet eighteen, the young artist from Málaga had produced a stunning body of work that ranged from dashed-off sketches to award-winning paintings. He had experienced happiness in the grandeur of the mountains, but he had also witnessed death, disease, rebellion, government repression, and decadence among Spain's poorest citizens. A prodigy and a trailblazer, these youthful experiences would shape and mold Picasso's personality—and his artistic creations—for the rest of his life.

Sadness, Pain, and the Blue Period

For Picasso, 1899 was a busy year both intellectually and creatively. Having rejected the traditional academic painting techniques taught in art school, Picasso dedicated himself to breaking the boundaries that had previously defined art. He rejected the view that artists strictly portray subjects as realistically as possible. Instead, he painted subjects with wavy or blurred lines, simplified contours, and nonrealistic colors.

Picasso was not the only one who rejected the traditional and embraced the experimental in Barcelona. His unique method of painting intersected neatly with a movement in art, literature, and philosophy called modernism. Members of the modernist community appreciated the progressive attitudes of northern European artists, philosophers, and writers, which contrasted sharply with the stuffy, conservative culture of Spain. Modernists had a high regard for German philosopher Friedrich Nietzsche, French poet Paul-Marie Verlaine, English writer Oscar Wilde, and German composer Richard Wagner. Artistically, modernists were inspired by the French art nouveau, or new art movement, a highly decorative style characterized by flowing curved lines and ornamental flower or plant patterns. Not limited to painting, the art nouveau style was also seen in architecture, furniture, glass, and illustration.

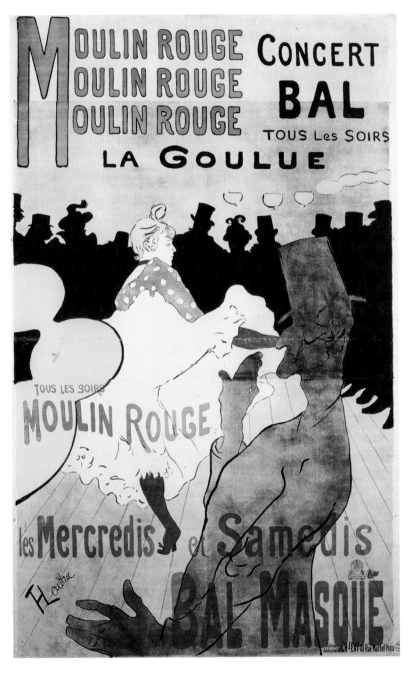

The style and subjects of Henri de Toulouse-Lautrec's work, such as the dancers depicted in bold, flowing colors in *Moulin Rouge: La Goulue,* were highly influential with Spanish modernists.

The art nouveau posters by French artist Henri de Toulouse-Lautrec were particularly influential among Spanish modernists. These large paintings of dancers at the Moulin Rouge cabaret in Paris capture the excitement and imagery of

MODERNISM

Modernism is a loosely defined art movement of the late nineteenth and early twentieth centuries that includes works of art, literature, graphic arts such as posters, and even puppet shows. In Barcelona, where Picasso was living, modernists embraced progressive international trends that stood in contrast to the conservative social climate of Spain. In terms of art, this included the use of symbolism, which emphasized mood and atmosphere over realistic depictions of subjects. Modernists revered the French art nouveau movement characterized by Henri de Toulouse-Lautrec. This French artist was known for his depictions of prostitutes and dancing girls painted with gracefully twisting contour lines, simplified shapes, and artificial colors. Toulouse-Lautrec's influence can be seen in Picasso's paintings from the early 1900s.

This elevation of the symbolic and rejection of traditional beliefs was considered a revolutionary act in the early twentieth century. It was seen by those in power as a denigration of revered traditions in religion, government, and culture. Modernists further inflamed authorities by committing themselves to political anarchy and expressing sympathy for the plight of the urban poor.

dancing by portraying the subjects with wavy, curvilinear lines and bright colors.

Toulouse-Lautrec's artwork was considered experimental and revolutionary at the time, especially because it often featured lively depictions of dancing girls, prostitutes, and others who were rejected by mainstream society. This positive portrayal of outsiders meshed with the modernist political philosophy, which rejected the religious institutions that dominated society. Instead, it embraced anarchy, or a total lack of government control over people's actions. The overall aims of the movement's members are described by one of the founding fathers of Spanish modernism, painter Santiago Rusiñol: "[Modernists aim] to extract life from the abnormal, the extraordinary, the outrageous; to express the horror of the rational mind as it contemplates the pit [death]. . . . We prefer to be symbolists and unstable, and even crazy and decadent, rather than fallen or meek. . . . Common sense oppresses us; there is too much cautiousness in our land."[18]

The Four Cats

While Picasso never pledged allegiance to the modernist movement, he was one of the few Barcelona artists with the creativity to make art that lived up to the modernist ideal. Although he was barely eighteen, Picasso's talents were instantly recognized by the modernists, and the young painter was drawn into their social circle at a beer hall called Els Quatre Gats, or The Four Cats. This tavern, modeled on a Parisian cabaret, was the hub for the Spanish modernist artists and writers who had visited Paris. In *Picasso: An Intimate Portrait*, poet and author Sabartés describes the attitudes of the patrons in The Four Cats: "We breathed an air infested with northern modernism. Nothing counted except the fashion from Paris. All our intellectuals had been to France."[19]

The Four Cats offered cheap food and drink and hosted art exhibitions, poetry readings, musical concerts, puppet shows, and theatrical productions. But the tavern was much more than a place for entertainment. According to Rusiñol:

[The Four Cats is an] inn for the disillusioned . . . a corner full of warmth for those who long for home . . . a museum for those who look for illuminations for the soul . . . a tavern . . . for those who love the shadow of butterflies and the essence of a cluster of grapes; a gothic beer-hall for lovers of the North, and [a Spanish] patio for lovers of the South . . . a place to cure the ills of our century, and a place for friendship and harmony.[20]

Pere Romeu, owner of The Four Cats, published the popular modernist magazine *Quatre Gats* and also displayed French art journals which were keenly perused by Picasso and other patrons. In late 1899 Romeu held a contest to decide who would design the advertisements, posters, menus, and leaflets for the bar. Picasso won and the sinuous lines and bright colors of the artwork he made for the commission shows the unmistakable influence of Toulouse-Lautrec. The art nouveau style is also a prominent feature in dozens of charcoal and watercolor portraits that Picasso produced of patrons at The Four Cats. The drawings include Picasso's close friends Sabartés and painter Carles Casagemas, along with Rusiñol, Ramon Casas, and Miquel Utrillo, painters who founded the modernist movement in Barcelona.

"An Artist from Head to Toe"

In February 1900 Picasso held his first major exhibition at The Four Cats, exhibiting about 150 drawings he made of his friends along with three oil paintings. Rather than present them in what was considered a respectable manner, according to Sabartés, Picasso wanted "to infuriate the public,"[21] and so tacked the unmounted and unframed pictures to the wall in a haphazard display.

Picasso's rebellious desire to inflame achieved its desired affect. Critic Sebastià Trullol i Plana writes that Picasso had "entered the world of art obsessed with the most extreme form of *modernismo* . . . [and is] madly in love with the *modernista* school, a lamentable confusion of artistic sense and a mistaken concept of art."[22] Another review in the progressive magazine *La Vanguardia* is not quite as negative, making concessions for the fact that Picasso was only eighteen years old, "almost a child . . . [who] shows extraordinary ease in the handling of his pencil and brush; he is a master, too, of that fundamental quality, graceful execution. . . . [However] as one examines the work carefully one notices mistakes [and] lack of experience."[23] Not all reviews criticized Picasso, however. One anonymous visitor writes in the guest book:

EXTRACTING EVERY LAST DROP OF MEANING

Within the space of a few months in late 1899 and early 1900, Picasso drew more than 150 portraits of the patrons of The Four Cats (Els Quatre Gats). As John Richardson explains in A Life of Picasso, the obsession to create the same type of picture over and over remained with Picasso his entire life:

The Quatre Gats portraits mark a turning point in Picasso's approach to work. Hitherto he had gone along with [his father's] strategy and envisaged his career in terms of successive set pieces that make successive splashes at major exhibitions. While "the big picture" would remain [a goal], he now embarked on a lifetime habit of working serially. He would seize on some subject or theme, devise an appropriately expressive idiom and abandon himself to its development. Just how this creative process functioned is a mystery that would puzzle him all his life. Sometimes, he said, he would exhaust the concept in the space of a sketchbook; sometimes he would return again and again to the attack over a period of months or years, until he had extracted every last drop of meaning, every last pictorial twist, from it.

John Richardson, *A Life of Picasso*, vol. 1. New York: Random House, 1991, p. 149.

[We] were delighted to look at more than 150 works, each one of them worthy of being a passport to the realm of art. . . . Picasso is an artist from head to toe. . . . In painting he is a revolutionary. . . . All his paintings are full of great strength and ease. . . . In each stroke of the pencil or of charcoal, in each brushstroke, one can see a profound faith in the art he is making. . . . [This] collection presents . . . a portrait of the present age.[24]

Parisian Pleasure Palaces

By the autumn of 1900, after "breathing air infested with north-ern modernism" as Sabartés says, perhaps it was inevitable that Picasso began making plans to move to Paris. This was the city where impressionist paintings by Édouard Manet, Claude Monet, Paul Cézanne, and others were displayed in salons, galleries, and museums. These impressionists had pioneered a new style of art. They did not paint subjects; they painted light, using pastels and bright, unmixed colors to create pictures that gave a simplified im-pression rather than a realistic view of a subject.

Picasso moved to Paris a few days before his nineteenth birthday in October. In a large art studio on Rue Gabrielle, partially financed by his parents, the young artist quickly be-gan assimilating the impressionist influences into his own work. As luck would have it, several days after his arrival Pi-casso chanced to meet an old friend from Barcelona, Pedro Mañach, who had left behind a lucrative family business in or-der to become a Paris art dealer specializing in young Spanish painters. Mañach visited Picasso's studio and was so impressed he offered the painter 150 francs a month (about $300 in 2006) for a given number of paintings to be supplied on de-mand. While this was no great fortune, the average French worker earned about the same amount, and it was enough to support Picasso's basic needs while he was gaining a foothold in the Parisian art world. In addition, Picasso painted so fast that it would not require a great deal of his time to meet Mañach's demands.

Casagemas and Pallarés soon arrived in Paris. The three young men were nearly inseparable, spending many nights vis-iting the Moulin Rouge and the Moulin de la Galette where dancers did the latest dance called the cancan. According to *Pablo Picasso: His Life and Times* by French art critic and author Pierre Cabanne, "Picasso liked the overheated, lust-laden muskiness of these pleasure palaces where formally dressed so-ciety people rubbed elbows . . . [with dancing] girls."[25] The pleasure palaces also provided artistic inspiration for Picasso, and his first Paris painting, *Dance at the Moulin de la Galette*,

Picasso's first painting after moving to Paris, *Dance at the Moulin de la Galette,* was inspired by the lively nightlife in the dancehalls he liked to visit.

was a tribute to Toulouse-Lautrec who would die within a year from alcoholism.

When not painting or visiting Parisian night spots, Picasso entertained with his friends at the Rue Gabrielle studio. The artists often invited pretty models to their parties, and soon three young women, Odette Lenoir, Antoinette Fornerod, and Germaine Gargallo, were spending a great deal of time with the Spaniards. Casagemas "fell violently and demandingly in love with Germaine," according to Cabanne, "but she returned the feeling only moderately."[26] Unable to deal with Germaine's indifference, Casagemas became extremely distraught and began drinking heavily. However, Casagemas's obsession with his unrequited love soon bored Picasso, whose passions were focused on painting, drawing, and sketching. And, as Cabanne writes, Picasso could create pictures of Paris nightlife as quickly as a camera takes a photo:

> Coming out of a cabaret at night, Pablo would see the sidewalk pleasure purveyors [prostitutes], go up to their rooms, and paint the girls in chemises. . . . [In] one quick nimble stroke, he caught a cancan dancer. . . . A woman went by, wearing a large hat, and in a pen stroke enhanced by color crayons, there she was. His eye was a recording machine that missed nothing. His hand, no less quick, set up the inventory of what his avid, lucid, and acute eye saw. . . . The girls were precisely portrayed, thin faces with pinched lips, coal-black eyes, "dog collar" around the neck, high chignon, long skirt and the disillusioned but promising air of the professionals of love for sale. Cutthroats and pickpockets under Pablo's pen flanked society ladies or the Eiffel Tower with a bottle of sparkling wine, symbol of Paris by night.[27]

Mañach sold the paintings produced in this manner—along with oils Picasso painted in his studio—to some of Paris's most elite tastemakers. One steady customer, gallery owner Berthe Weill, exclaimed "Nobody wanted anything but Picasso's!"[28] She resold Picasso's paintings for more than two times what Mañach was paying the young genius every month. Most notably, Weill sold *Dance at the Moulin de la Galette* to Paris publisher and art patron Arthur Huc for 250 francs, making this painting Picasso's first to enter a prestigious French collection.

The Death of Casagemas

In December 1900 Picasso decided to leave Paris and travel back to Spain where he visited family members in Barcelona and

Málaga. Rather than return to Paris, Picasso moved to Madrid in February 1901 although he had no job or artistic prospects. Living in poverty, Picasso painted by the light of a single candle in a garret with no heat in the midst of an especially freezing winter. Living in this miserable condition, Picasso learned that Casagemas had committed suicide after being jilted by Germaine, shooting himself in the head in a Paris restaurant as she watched in horror with several other friends. Picasso blamed himself, feeling that if he had stayed in Paris or paid more attention to his friend's depression, the suicide could have been prevented. These feelings dredged up memories of Conchita's death in 1895.

Picasso created a series of paintings featuring Casagemas, according to Huffington, "to exorcise the pain and guilt that his friend's death had stirred in him."[29] The first *Death of Casagemas* appeared in the young man's obituary in an art magazine, portraying Casagemas lying in his coffin with a small bullet hole in his temple.

Despite his grief, Picasso could not escape from his responsibilities—Mañach was demanding that the artist return to Paris to provide paintings according to the terms of their formal agreement. In May 1901 Mañach arranged for the nineteen-year-old Picasso to take over the Paris studio formerly used by Casagemas, located next door to the restaurant where he had killed himself. Mañach also introduced Picasso to Ambroise Vollard, a shrewd art dealer with an elite clientele of wealthy investors and influential museums. Vollard immediately offered Picasso a show at his gallery which would be sure to attract reviews in major Paris publications.

Picasso had only three weeks to prepare for the exhibition, but most of the sixty-four paintings that were shown were produced during that short time. Unlike his exhibition at The Four Cats, reviewers were unanimous in their praises for the brash young painter who took his inspiration from Parisian street scenes. Writing for the widely read *Le Journal*, critic Gustave Coquiot states:

> Here we have a new harmonist of bright tonalities, with dazzling tones of red, yellow, green and blue. We

realize at once that P.R. Picasso wants to see and express everything. . . . [His] paintings of women, landscapes, street scenes, interiors, workmen, etc., etc., represent life precisely as we live it today; while tomorrow, we can be sure, he will give us all the other things, which, being now little more than a child, he has not yet had time to accomplish. . . . Here are all the happy, mischievous little girls in exquisite pink and grey, with their wild dances and fluttering skirts; and here are the little boys crouching forgotten beside a sandpit, playing gravely and clumsily, with comical faces . . . or with cunning, wide awake expressions like monkeys. . . . Such, at the present time, is the work of Pablo Ruiz Picasso—an artist who paints all round the clock, who never believes that the day is over, in a city that offers a different spectacle every minute.[30]

A Period of Grief, Sadness, and Wretchedness

The exhibition provided Picasso with his first financial success as Vollard sold more than half the works, with commissions paid to the artist rather than Mañach. In addition, the show brought Picasso commissions for posters and magazine illustrations. However, the dazzling impressionist reds and yellows mentioned by Coquiot would soon be abandoned by the artist. In October 1901, still obsessed with Casagemas's suicide, Picasso painted *Evocation (The Burial of Casagemas)* using only somber shades of blue and muted bluish browns and greens. This monochromatic painting marks the beginning of what is now called Picasso's Blue Period, which features not only pictures of Casagemas but other depressing subjects such as blind beggars, women prisoners, and diseased prostitutes. Sabartés describes conversations he had with Picasso during the Blue Period that explain the artist's motivation to paint society's victims:

Picasso believes that art emanates from sadness and pain. . . . That sadness lends itself to meditation, and that grief is at the depths of life. We are passing through . . . a period of uncertainty which everyone considers from the point of view of his own wretchedness. And since our life is passing through a period of grief, sadness and of wretchedness, life, with all its torments, constitutes the very foundation of his theory of art.[31]

THE IMPRESSIONISTS

Like most other painters in the early twentieth century Picasso was influenced by impressionism, a style pioneered by Édouard Manet in the 1860s. In The World of Picasso, *Lael Wertenbaker explores the impressionist style:*

*A*cademic painters held fast to prescriptions for composition, perspective and color that had ruled art since the Renaissance [in the fifteenth century]. But an artistic revolution had been gathering force ever since the 1860s, when Édouard Manet first shattered certain Renaissance conventions. He dared to paint the female nude in everyday settings rather than as an idealized Venus [goddess]. . . . [The] artists who followed him took further liberties with both technique and subject matter. The Impressionists of the 1870s disregarded conventional modeling altogether, and instead aimed at capturing the ephemeral effects of light. They used bright colors instead of the somber hues of the traditional masters, and a new kind of dappled brushwork of small, quick strokes.

Lael Wertenbaker, *The World of Picasso.* Alexandria, VA: Time-Life, 1967, pp. 29–30.

Two Women at a Bar, with its depiction of its subjects as huddled and forlorn, is typical of Picasso's Blue Period, in which his work reflected his despair and sadness following Casagemas's burial.

Restive, lonely, and depressed, Picasso broke his contract with Mañach in early 1902 and moved back to Barcelona, hoping to find comfort with his family. Although he returned to the thriving social milieu at The Four Cats, Picasso continued to paint gloomy monochromatic scenes of alienation. Unlike many artists, however, Picasso's melancholy did not stopper his creativity, and he continued to paint at an unrelenting pace.

In Paris, Weill held several exhibitions of Picasso's works which were favorably reviewed for their dark, emotional content. As reviewer Thilda Harlor writes about a November 1902 exhibit: "We see three studies of women, like cameos showing painful reality, dedicated to misery, loneliness, and exhaustion. A fierce light surrounds these creatures. There is a violent play of light and shade above and around them. One woman in particular personifies despair, isolation amid the unfeeling consolations of nature."[32]

Picasso's sadness lasted throughout 1903 during which time he painted some of the most celebrated paintings of his Blue Period. Many of the subjects are crouched or hunched over guitars or drinks in a barroom. The human figures in these paintings lack what Wertenbaker calls the "astounding precision" Picasso learned in art school. Instead they are "distorted imaginatively . . . in order to convey the moral and physical decay of [their] characters. He drew elongated limbs and fingers, painted bony, fleshless bodies, and adopted stylized, sexless profiles."[33] In this manner, Picasso created his own style for the first time, no longer relying on impressionists or art nouveau painters for insight. Meanwhile, the Paris art world was taking notice of the brilliant young Spanish artist, and they were willing to pay ever increasing prices for his work. By the time The Four Cats went out of business in the summer of 1903, it was becoming apparent to Picasso that his life was at a crossroads. Barcelona had little more to offer, and he could not dwell on the death of Casagemas indefinitely. At the age of twenty-one, he had brought his unbending vision of blue to a world where compromise was the norm. It was time to take the next step and move to Paris permanently.

3

Love and Roses

By April 1904, after several restless years spent moving back and forth between Spain and France, Picasso finally settled in Paris. Although he had developed a reputation as an audacious artist acclaimed by critics, money continued to elude the young artist. Picasso lived in poverty in a studio located at 13 Rue Ravignan, in Montmartre, a hilly neighborhood that was the artistic center of Paris at the turn of the century. The studio was in a rundown building known as the Bateau-Lavoir, or laundry boat. The building was so named because its shape resembled a type of barge laundresses used to wash clothes in the Seine River. Sweltering in the summer and frigid in the winter, Picasso's studio was sparsely furnished with an old mattress, a trunk, a single cane chair, a table, and an easel. A small woodstove provided heat, and a ceramic bowl sat atop the stove for use as a bathroom sink. The only running water in the building came from a single cold-water tap in the basement that was shared by the two dozen or so tenants living in the twelve studios.

In Picasso's studio dozens of Blue Period paintings were piled on every surface including the bed and in the bathtub. As Cabanne writes, "the blue paintings of paupers, gaunt sad streetgirls . . . blind men, old people in rags, [and] hungry children"[34] added to the dejected atmosphere.

Drawn to Picasso

Picasso was not the only poor artist at the Bateau-Lavoir. The building had previously been home to famed impressionist painter Pierre-Auguste Renoir during his early career, and Picasso's neighbors included Barcelona sculptor Paco Durrio, painters Ramón Pichot and Manolo, and struggling French

Fernande Olivier, depicted here in *Seated Nude,* served as both a model and a muse for Picasso's work after his return to Paris.

artists and models. One resident in particular, Fernande Olivier, caught Picasso's artistic eye. She was living in Bateau-Lavoir with sculptor Gaston de Labaum. Picasso had tried to talk to her several times, only to be ignored. However, on August 4, 1904, during a torrential rainstorm, Olivier could no longer disregard Picasso. She rushed in from outdoors soaked to the skin and found the artist standing in the hallway holding a wet kitten he had just rescued from the storm. Picasso blocked Olivier's path and thrust the kitten into her arms. They both laughed and Olivier accompanied the painter to his studio where she was impressed with the work, writing in her autobiography *Loving Picasso*, "I find something morbid in them, which is quite disturbing, but I also feel drawn to them."[35] She was horrified by Picasso's apartment, however, with its cobwebs, cigarette burns in the furniture, dirt on the floor, and the strong smell of animals from the artist's tame white mouse and two dogs he kept as pets. Despite her initial reservations, Olivier and Picasso soon began a love affair.

Olivier was born Fernande Bellevallée in June 1881, four months before Picasso. By the time she met Picasso, she was a successful model who posed for several artists, and, as Mailer writes, she was "tall, red-headed, and beautiful; she stood out vividly in their impoverished bohemian circle."[36] Little wonder that Picasso was smitten with Olivier to the point that he began to ignore his work when she was nearby. Writing in her diary, Olivier describes the artist's dedication to her:

He adores me with real sincerity, which I find touching. . . . [He] is sweet, intelligent . . . and he drops everything for me. His eyes plead with me, and he keeps everything I leave behind as if it were a holy relic. If I fall asleep, he's beside the bed when I wake up, his eyes anxiously fixed on me. He doesn't see his friends anymore, doesn't work anymore, stays out in the square so as to catch sight of me more quickly and more often. He's asking me to come and live with him, and I don't know what I should do.[37]

A LOVER'S IMPRESSION OF PICASSO

Fernande Olivier was Picasso's first girlfriend and a great source of inspiration during the artist's Rose Period. Olivier described her first impressions of Picasso in her diary which was later turned into the book Loving Picasso:

I've mentioned the Spanish painter who lives in our building. Well, for some time now I've been bumping into him wherever I go, and he looks at me with his huge deep eyes, sharp but brooding, full of suppressed fire. I don't find him particularly attractive, but his strangely intense gaze forces me to look at him in return, although I've never answered him when he tries to make conversation. I don't know where to place him on the social scale and I can't tell how old he is. His mouth has a lovely shape, which makes him look young—while the deep lines from his nose to the corners of his mouth make him look old. The heavy nose with broad nostrils makes the face a little coarse, but everything about him suggests a powerful and deeply spiritual personality. Even when his lips are laughing, his eyes remain serious, and the pupils seem to be steeped in an inexpressible melancholy. His gestures are tentative, suggesting the kind of shyness that may conceal pride.

Fernande Olivier, *Loving Picasso*. New York: Henry N. Abrams, 2001, pp. 137, 139.

Olivier finally did move in with Picasso in September 1905, but until that time she was faced with the delicate task of seeing Picasso surreptitiously while living off and on with the jealous Labaum. Meanwhile, Olivier became Picasso's muse and nearly the sole subject of the artwork he created during that period. His sketchbook quickly filled with portraits of her, such as *The Actor* and *The Lovers (Fernande and Picasso)*, made when they first met. However, Picasso too showed his jealous side and soon forbade Olivier from modeling for other artists. With little else to do,

Olivier spent her days and nights lying in bed, sleeping so much that Picasso began to complain. As she slept, however, Picasso worked feverishly into the night, sometimes until six o'clock in the morning, painting watercolors such as *The Artist Watching Fernande Asleep.*

Picasso's *Child and Seated Saltimbanque* is representative of his Rose Period, in which his work frequently depicted circus artists and street performers and featured lighter, brighter colors.

Adding Colors

During these early months with Olivier, new colors such as chalky red hues and earth tones including yellow, brown, beige, and green began brightening Picasso's oil paintings. Picasso never explained why he switched from the monochromatic blues of the earlier years to these new colors, except to jokingly say he exhausted his supply of blue paint. Critics and biographers, however, point to several factors, including the artist's newest subject matter. Besides Olivier, Picasso was painting acrobats, musicians, harlequins, and clowns who performed in the Médrano Circus located in the Montmartre.

These entertainers, along with street acrobats and traveling circus artists known as *saltimbanques*, were often subjects in French poems and paintings, depicted as symbols of misery and social alienation. However, Picasso's newest friend, poet, writer, and art critic Guillaume Apollinaire described the *saltimbanques* as mysterious and enchanting. This was said to inspire Picasso to paint the circus people in a more positive light during what would come to be called his Rose Period.

Apollinaire, born in Italy to a Polish mother in 1880, came into Picasso's life around the same time as Olivier. Fluent in French, he was a talented writer and speaker, which made him a leading character among the bohemians in Paris.

Another influence on Picasso's art during the Rose Period is one that the artist refused to discuss. However, Olivier writes in her diary that she and Picasso smoked opium for three days in the summer of 1905, an experience that she claimed helped her achieve "a spiritual intensity and sharpening of intellectual awareness ... [making] everything seem so beautiful, bright, and good."[38]

Whether or not drugs motivated Picasso during this time, his palette did brighten. Several of his paintings show happy *saltimbanques* in warm domestic circumstances, posing with babies, children, and pets. However, despite the bright colors, the foremost painting of the Rose Period, the large *Family of Saltimbanques*, depicts a vagabond troupe in a desolate setting and continues with the theme of alienation prominent during the Blue Period.

One figure in *Family of Saltimbanques*, the harlequin, represents a comic character who is agile and acrobatic. A character of myth and legend, the harlequin is also a prankster who likes to play jokes on people, disobeys the normal conventions of society, and uses wine to entice women. *Family of Saltimbanques* is one of the first of Picasso's works that depicts a harlequin, but the character would reappear time and time again. It is said to be Picasso's alter ego; that is, his second personality, or another persona within him.

Picasso broke from the *saltimbanques* he frequently depicted during his Rose Period to paint *Boy with a Pipe*. He is said to have added the rose garland on the boy's head on a "whim."

Boy with a Pipe

Not all of Picasso's subject matter concerns circus people during the early Rose Period. He continued to paint portraits, and one of the most iconic paintings of that era, *Garçon à la pipe* or *Boy with a Pipe*, was made in December 1905. Poet, writer, and art critic André Salmon, one of Picasso's best friends at the time, describes the painting and the circumstances surrounding its creation:

After a delightful series of metaphysical [abstract] acrobats, dancers . . . clowns and wistful Harlequins, Picasso had painted, without a model, the purest and simplest image of a young Parisian working boy, beardless and in blue overalls: having indeed, more or less the same appearance as the artist himself during working hours. One night, Picasso abandoned the company of his friends and their intellectual chit-chat. He returned to his studio, took the canvas he had abandoned a month before and crowned the figure of the little apprentice lad with roses. He had made this work a masterpiece thanks to a sublime whim.[39]

A Poet's Influence

During Picasso's Rose Period he spent countless hours discussing philosophy with his friend, poet Guillaume Apollinaire. In A Life of Picasso *John Richardson describes Apollinaire's influence on Picasso and his work:*

𝒜pollinaire would be a constant solace [who provided steady encouragement] to Picasso. He opened up his imagination to a vast new range of intellectual stimuli: to new concepts of black humor, to the pagan past. . . . Apollinaire . . . had no difficulty converting Picasso to . . . his definition of art as "the perpetual immoral subversion of the existing order." Apollinaire encouraged Picasso to . . . picture himself in different roles: the self-dramatizing role of a saltimbanque, strolling player or circus performer, the picturesque outcast at odds with conventional society; or the more [mysterious] role of harlequin, the player of tricks that alarm and mystify as well as entertain. . . . Apollinaire exerted an immeasurable influence on Picasso's imagination and intellect, but the only time he left any overt imprint on his subject was when they were both preoccupied with harlequins. . . . So similar is their imagery that it sometimes seems as if the painter and the poet had access to the same imagination. Indeed the Rose period . . . could as well be renamed the Apollinaire period. . . . [The] series of thirteen engravings—mostly saltimbanque subjects—that Picasso began toward the end of 1904 look as if they were intended as his illustrations to Apollinaire's poems.

John Richardson, *A Life of Picasso*, vol. 1. New York: Random House, 1991, p. 334.

Although it would have been impossible for the poverty-stricken Picasso to imagine at the time, the painting he created on a whim has entered the record books. On May 5, 2004, *Boy with a Pipe* sold for a record $104.2 million at a Sotheby's auction in New York City.

Sessions with Stein

While Picasso certainly did not become a millionaire in 1906, his fortunes did improve. Apollinaire was part of a social circle that included influential American author and critic Gertrude Stein, who, along with her husband Leo, was an art collector. Stein held regular salons, or gatherings of prominent people, in her home. Stein's salons attracted a wide range of renowned artists, writers, and intellectuals. It was there that Picasso met the great French impressionist Henri Matisse in 1906, and the two artists would remain what Cabanne calls "friendly enemies, watching each other, sniffing critically, spitting sarcasms and double entendres, and both actually rather enjoying the fun of it."[40] As they aged, the two artists became better friends, often visiting each other's studio, commenting on works in progress, and exchanging paintings.

In addition to providing a social milieu where Picasso could meet legendary artists, Stein also became his patron. The first work she acquired was *Harlequin's Family with an Ape*, one of the many paintings of *saltimbanques* of this period. When not buying major works, Stein demonstrated her friendship to Picasso by purchasing his random sketches for the equivalent of twenty dollars. She also reluctantly let Picasso paint her portrait. She came to rue the decision when Picasso made her pose for the picture day after day. During these sessions, Picasso carefully painted, or as Richardson writes, "wrestled on canvas with Gertrude as if she were a sphinx whose image held the key to the future of his art."[41]

Even after ninety grueling sittings at Bateau-Lavoir, Picasso did not finish *Portrait of Gertrude Stein*. Finally, near the end of 1906 he completed the work in a single night without the model present. When Stein's friends grumbled that the picture did not look like her, Picasso remarked "Everybody thinks she is not at all like her portrait but never mind, in the end she will manage to look just like it."[42] This remark proved to be prophetic, for everyone who knew Stein agreed that by the time she died in 1946, she had come to look remarkably like Picasso's portrait.

The Atmosphere of the Country

Stein was not the only person who saw the value of Picasso's work. In April 1906 Vollard, who had exhibited Picasso's paintings in 1901, purchased almost all of the artist's recent paintings for two thousand gold francs. This was a virtual fortune worth about four thousand dollars, or 150 times Picasso's average monthly income at that time. Picasso used this money to take Olivier to meet his old friends in Barcelona in May 1906. Later the couple vacationed for the rest of the summer in Gósol, a remote village untouched by civilization, in Spain's Pyrenees Mountains. There, the colors in Picasso's palette changed once again. While creating dozens of nudes, sun-drenched landscapes, still lifes, and portraits, he incorporated thick clay-like browns, taupes, yellows, and reds. In addition to drawing and painting, Picasso began to sculpt, chiseling away at blocks of boxwood to create *Bois de Gósol* (Wood of Gósol) and several other sculptures.

During this productive and idyllic time in the Pyrenees, Picasso's mood lifted, and he seemed to be enjoying life for the first time, as Olivier writes:

Pablo is quite different in Spain. He's more cheerful, not so wild, more sparkling and animated, and he takes a calmer,

Picasso portrayed his American author and art-collector friend in *Portrait of Gertrude Stein.*

WE SURRENDERED OURSELVES BODY AND SOUL

Although Picasso struggled financially during his early years in Paris, he refused to compromise his artistic vision for monetary gain. The artist made his philosophy clear to his friend and biographer Jaime Sabartés in Picasso: An Intimate Portrait:

[**W**hen] we (Picasso and his . . . friends) used to make our constructions, we produced "pure truth," without pretensions, without tricks, without malice. What we did then had never been done before: we did it disinterestedly, and if it is worth anything it is because we did it without expecting to profit from it. . . . We put enthusiasm into the work, and this alone, even if that were all that were in it, would be enough: and much more than is usually put into an effort—for we surrendered ourselves to it completely, body and soul. We departed so far from the modes of expression then known and appreciated that we felt safe from any suspicion of mercenary aims.

Jaime Sabartés, *Picasso: An Intimate Portrait.* New York: Prentice, 1948, p. 212.

more balanced view of things. He seems to be at ease. He glows with happiness, so unlike the kind of person he is in Paris, where shy and inhibited, as if the atmosphere is alien to him. I've never met anyone less suited to life in Paris. . . . The atmosphere of his own country seems to inspire him, and there is much stronger emotion and sensitivity in these drawings than anything he has done in Paris.[43]

Two Massive Figures

When Picasso returned to Paris in mid-August 1906, he continued to work in three dimensions, modeling clay sculptures fired in the Bateau-Lavoir studio of his friend, sculptor Paco Durrio. In the months that followed, Picasso's oil paintings also began to take on a sculptural look; that is, his subjects took on a three-dimensional, solid, angular appearance in contrast to the flat, wispy figures of his Rose and Blue periods.

A prime example of this new style is seen in *Two Nudes*. This painting is part of a series of figure studies that Picasso began around 1902. *Two Nudes* shows two women standing facing each other before a curtain. In *Picasso: The Early Years*, art history professor Margaret Werth describes the sculptural qualities of *Two Nudes*:

> Two massive figures are crammed into the space of the picture, their cone-shaped breasts, the abbreviated modeling of their legs, torsos, and arms, and their massive breadth locating them in a world of . . . volume and, to some degree, mass. Both figures flex their arms, gesturing toward themselves, touching themselves, and displaying muscular forearms. . . . Entry into the picture—and also any imagined entry through the curtain into the potential space beyond—is blocked by the massive squat bodies that push against the four sides of the picture, pressing its limits. The two figures bear down on the viewer, confrontational rather than seductive.[44]

The sculptural look of this period was also influenced by a show Picasso had viewed at the legendary Louvre art museum in Paris. The exhibition consisted of ancient sculptures from the fifth century B.C. that had recently been excavated in southern Spain, near

Picasso's *Two Nudes* represents his foray into creating figures with shapes and stances influenced by his work and interest in sculpture.

Picasso's hometown. While these sculptures were of minor historical interest to the general public, Picasso revered them as being among the few examples of primeval Spanish artwork. Although they were smaller and more crudely made than ancient sculptures found in Greece and elsewhere, Picasso was fascinated by them because, according to Richardson, "the artist was anxious to demolish traditional [standards] of beauty."[45]

The Louvre exhibition was but one example of sculpture in the ancient style that inspired Picasso. One night in late 1906 Matisse was attending a dinner with Picasso at Stein's, and after dinner he brought out an African statuette that he had acquired. Max Jacob, a confidant of Picasso's, continues the story:

> Matisse took a black wooden statuette off a table showed it to Picasso. Picasso held it in his hands all evening. The next morning, when I came to [Picasso's] studio, the floor was strewn with sheets of drawing paper. Each sheet had virtually the same drawing on it, a big woman's face with a single eye, a nose too long that merged into the mouth, a lock of hair on the shoulder.[46]

Picasso was headed off in a unique direction, alone among the great artists of the time. Working like a man possessed, he was preparing to make a major artistic statement, unique, shocking, and wonderful. When he was finished, the world of art, or the world in general, would be forever changed. But this was just the beginning for a twenty-five-year-old artist with a new vision for a new century.

Creating Cubism

By 1907 Picasso had achieved more in his twenty-five years than most artists could dream of. His dealer Vollard was selling his paintings nearly as fast as Picasso could produce them. His girlfriend Fernande Olivier was regarded as one of the most beautiful women in Paris. And Picasso was considered a superstar among the painters, intellectuals, and writers who flocked to his studio to laugh, drink, and watch the master at work. In Paris, only impressionist Henri Matisse was more famous. Although Picasso was not yet internationally famous, his paintings from the Blue and Rose periods were attracting attention from rich art lovers in Germany, Russia, and elsewhere.

It would not have been surprising for an artist in Picasso's position to continue producing rosy portraits, stylish nudes, and paintings of harlequins to appease collector's demands. However, Picasso was driven not by the marketplace but by a desire to create paintings unlike any the world had ever seen. His work was taking a radical turn, and some who viewed his new creations considered them grotesque, disturbing, and even loathsome.

"Around Him Are His Monsters"

In the spring of 1907, Picasso could be found working furiously in his studio at Bateau-Lavoir, making sketches in charcoal, pencil, pastels (colored chalk), watercolor, and oil. In nearly one hundred sketches, he created figures with disjointed features that are both repulsive and strangely attractive. Cabanne describes this new art:

> Picasso paints. Around him are his monsters, women with unhealthy flesh, Negroid heads with broadly striated cheeks, masks shaped as by scythe strokes with empty sockets, pink and gray nudes strong as tree trunks. . . . [They] were geometrical constructs, with unbelievable faces and erratic arms, a [confusion] of shapes going every which way, looking like nothing, reminiscent of nothing known, unless perhaps the targets in carnival games of skill. The bodies with their broad flesh-pink planes were not shaded . . . but chiseled with frigid violence, unrestrained fury. Here and there, on each disjointed torso, a terrifying mask with madwoman's eyes.[47]

One day, taking a break during this maelstrom of creativity, Picasso visited the Museum of Comparative Sculpture located in the Palace of the Trocadéro near the Eiffel Tower. After viewing the sculpture, Picasso wandered into the Ethnological Museum, which was filled with ancient African masks and statues, called fetishes, said to have supernatural powers. Although the dark, musty room assaulted his senses, Picasso was attracted to the antique religious icons. Many were created by African shamans, or spiritual leaders, who used the fetishes to aid communication with mystical spirits in order to attract luck, heal the sick, and ward off evil. Picasso was both repelled and attracted by the magical significance of these objects, as he later told author and French minister of culture André Malraux:

> I was all alone. I wanted to get away. But I didn't leave. I stayed. I stayed. I understood that it was very important: something was happening to me, right? The masks weren't

just like any other pieces of sculpture. Not at all. They were magic things.... They were against everything—against unknown, threatening spirits.... I understood; I too am against everything. I too believe that everything is unknown, that everything is an enemy! Everything! Not the details—women, children, babies, tobacco, playing—but the whole of it! I understood what the Negroes used their sculpture for.... They were weapons. To help people avoid coming under the influence of spirits again, to help them become independent. They're tools. If we give spirits a form, we become independent. I understood why I was a painter.[48]

With this revelation, Picasso went back to his studio and incorporated the masks into his new sketches. He gave those spirits their form and so became independent.

The Young Ladies of Avignon

In the early summer of 1907, Picasso prepared a canvas almost 8 feet (2.4m) square, the largest he had ever made. He began to paint angular nudes of five prostitutes posed in a brothel like one he had visited on Avignon Street in Barcelona. Each of the figures in the work, called *Les Demoiselles d'Avignon* or *The Young Ladies of Avignon*, is different from the other. The face of the subject on the extreme left of the painting has the most realistic face with almond eyes and black hair. Moving to the right, the faces of the figures become more abstract and elongated. The eyes are not realistically human, but are painted at uneven angles, and they seem to be glazed over from the effects of smoking opium. The noses resemble

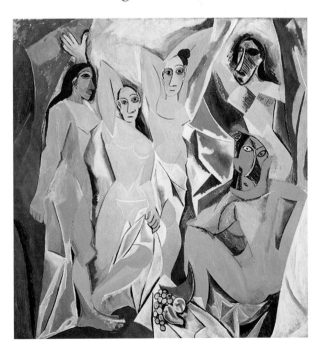

The abstract, distorted portrayals of five prostitutes in *The Young Ladies of Avignon* was influenced by Picasso's interest in ancient African masks.

"Picasso Simply Smashed the Body to Bits"

When Picasso painted Les Demoiselles d'Avignon, *the primitive and brutal imagery in the painting received almost universal condemnation. In* The World of Picasso, *Lael Wertenbaker explains why many believed the artist had gone too far:*

What shook them was the extent of Picasso's daring. As a declaration of independence [from] existing values, the *Demoiselles* was—even for an era familiar with experiment—an extraordinary manifesto. It did violence to almost every [rule] of Western painting, recent as well as traditional. Above all it did violence to the human form. Picasso simply smashed the body to bits . . . then put the pieces together again in a startling [grouping] of angular planes, rounded wedges, facets of every shape. . . . [He] further defied anatomical principle by discarding ears, placing eyes at different levels, and presenting noses in profile on faces seen from the front.

Lael Wertenbaker, *The World of Picasso.* Alexandria, VA: Time-Life, 1967, p. 54.

isosceles triangles, what French critics labeled *quart-de-Brie*, or wedges of Brie cheese. On the right side of the painting, the two women seem to have animalistic masks as faces.

The bodies in *Demoiselles* seem half-finished, an afterthought of jutting, pointed knees, elbows, and squared-off breasts. Thomas Hoving, former director of the Metropolitan Museum of Modern Art (MOMA) in New York, describes first seeing the picture as a young man: "The painting exploded in my eyes like some kind of pink, blue, and beige bomb."[49]

Playing with Perspective

Another shocking aspect of *Demoiselles* is its distortion of perspective. French painter Paul Cézanne began manipulating perspective in the mid-1880s. Before that time, artists envisioned an invisible vanishing point in their work. Using techniques developed during the Renaissance in the 1400s, painters directed lines and shadows toward the vanishing point to give paintings the illusion of depth on a flat two-dimensional canvas. Cézanne, however, believed that because people had two eyes and could swivel their heads, they could see objects from several perspectives at once. Therefore, he

Paul Cézanne experimented with perspective in works such as *Still Life with Pitcher and Eggplant.*

created paintings such as *Still Life with Plate of Cherries*, in which the cherries are seen from above, other fruit is seen from the front, and the tablecloth seems to be in several dimensions at once.

Cézanne was virtually unknown until 1905 when there was a large exhibit of his work in Paris, attended by Picasso and other young artists who were electrified by his work. Before he died the next year, Cézanne expressed the belief that everything in nature could be painted "in terms of the cylinder, the sphere, and the cone."[50] This quote, along with his unique vision of perspective, inspired Picasso to remark that "[Cézanne is] the father of us all."[51]

Perspective Is a "Ghastly Mistake"

While creating *Demoiselles*, Picasso embraced Cézanne's concepts of geometry and space. And, as he had in previous years, he seemed to relish the idea of thumbing his nose at four centuries of artistic tradition, commenting to painter Georges Braque, "The whole Renaissance tradition is antipathetic [hostile] to me. The hard-and-fast rules of perspective, which it succeeded in imposing on art, were a ghastly mistake."[52]

Throughout the intense, exhausting months when Picasso was creating *Demoiselles*, he let no one except Olivier into his studio. Finally, in July 1907 the artist unveiled the painting for Gertrude and Leo Stein. After looking upon the violently distorted, primitive bodies in stunned silence, Leo joked "You've been trying to paint the fourth dimension. How amusing!"[53] Gertrude later said that she thought Picasso was on a self-destructive path and was "finished."[54] When Matisse viewed the painting, he took it as a personal insult that mocked impressionism, swearing that he would make Picasso pay for this affront. Braque reacted more dramatically, telling Picasso "[It's] as if you were making us eat cotton waste or swallow gasoline so we can spit fire!"[55]

While it is difficult to imagine people reacting so strongly to a painting today, at that time no one had ever seen anything like Picasso's *Demoiselles*, which went far beyond Cézanne's ex-

PAUL CÉZANNE: THE FATHER OF CUBISM

Although Picasso is credited with inventing cubism, he was inspired by French painter Paul Cézanne who created paintings based on cubist concepts beginning in the 1880s. Nancy Doyle explains Cézanne's role in the development of cubism in "Artist Profile: Paul Cézanne":

Cezanne's great contribution was that he invented a new kind of space in painting. In the 400 years prior to the late 19th century, space in painting was Renaissance space—which was . . . linear perspective, trying to depict the illusion of space [height, width, and depth] on a two-dimensional surface. [Renaissance artists believed the] canvas was like a window looking out onto the real world, with parallel lines meeting at a point on the horizon line. After 1850, certain artists . . . began to gradually see the canvas not as a window on the world, but its own world, with its own laws. They did not want to depict space in terms of perspective, but more as a flat surface. . . . Also, instead of the chiaroscuro (light and dark shading) from the Renaissance, they used color . . . to depict volumes and space. Cezanne carried this further by . . . [melding] both the Renaissance notion of deep space, with the modern notion of the flat surface. This combining caused his paintings to have both flatness and three-dimensional space.

Nancy Doyle, "Artist Profile: Paul Cézanne," Nancy Doyle Fine Art, 2004. www.ndoylefineart.com/cezanne.html.

periments with perspective. As Wertenbaker writes, "Picasso demolished perspective. There is no depth in his figures; they do not occupy a rational position in rational space. . . . [His] distortion of face and figure . . . force the viewer to look everywhere at once."[56]

Stunned by the response from people he respected, Picasso rolled up his canvas and put it away. *Demoiselles* was not seen again until 1925. By this time, people were beginning to understand what the artist had created. As Richardson writes: "*Les Demoiselles d'Avignon* is the first unequivocally [unmistakably] twentieth-century masterpiece, a principal detonator of the modern [art] movement, the cornerstone of twentieth-century art. For Picasso it would also be a rite of passage: what he called an 'exorcism.' *The Demoiselles* cleared the way for cubism."[57]

Geometric Schemes and Cubes

The term *cubism* did not exist in 1907 and would not come into existence until the next year when Braque began to imitate Picasso. Although he had compared viewing *Demoiselles* to drinking gasoline, after that bitter experience Braque went back to his studio and began to experiment with angular distortions of the human figure. Braque painted *Grand Nu* in late 1907, a nude based on one of the figures in *Demoiselles*. In 1908 he painted six other pictures of figures, buildings, and landscapes. These pictures have little detail, and every object is represented by chunky blocks and

Houses on a Hill is one of several cubist landscapes that Picasso created.

cylinders. When this work was exhibited at a Paris gallery, visitors shrieked with laughter at the bizarre cube-like paintings. Art critic Louis Vauxcelles wrote a scathing review saying Braque had reduced "everything—skies, figures and houses—to geometric schemes, to *cubes.*"[58] Vauxcelles called the work "cubist" and, although it was meant as something of an insult, the phrase was quickly picked up by the Paris art community.

While Braque was creating his cubist landscapes, Picasso continued painting with distorted perspective, squared-off outlines, and few details. In 1909, while visiting Horta de San Juan, Spain, with Olivier, Picasso painted what is considered his first thoroughly cubist work. The picture *Houses on a Hill* is not a representation of a Spanish village but a jumble of blocks, rectangles, triangles, and pyramids depicted in shades of brown, greenish blue, and gray. A single window and several doorways are the only details, and even the clouds are square and flat. In "Cubism, a History and an Analysis, 1907–1914," abstract artist and author John Golding analyzes *Houses on a Hill* and several other cubist landscapes Picasso made at the time:

> Trees and natural forms are here almost completely eliminated. . . . Color is even more limited than before, and the palette for the [later] years is established: some of the paintings are in earth colors, grays and blacks, with a few touches of dull green, while others are in softer gray-blues and buffs. In all the paintings the deviations from traditional perspective . . . are carried to new lengths. Not only is there no central vanishing point, but the perspective, rather than being convergent is actually divergent, so that the rooftops and sides of the buildings are often broadest at their furthest ends. . . . The sky, too, is treated as a series of planes continuing the composition up to the top of the canvas, so that there is very little suggestion of depth even behind the buildings and mountains on the horizon.[59]

These paintings have come to be called analytical cubism, in which the subjects are analyzed in their most basic, segmented parts. For example, a village on a hillside would be represented only by squares and planes. Wertenbaker explains: "These parts were then spread on the canvas for analysis . . . and looked at from several angles and under varying conditions of light. . . . [Color] was essentially limited to monochrome—first browns or greens, later grays. Picasso may have wanted to avoid the distraction of colors in his analysis of form."[60]

Remove All Traces of Reality

While Picasso's cubist paintings were not widely praised, the artist found a new benefactor. In September 1909 wealthy Russian businessman Sergei Shchukin bought fifty of Picasso's paintings all at once, most of them from the Blue and Rose periods. With the small fortune he received from Shchukin, Picasso's days as a starving artist were at an end. He moved from Bateau-Lavoir to 11 Boulevard de Clichy into a large apartment with a comfortable living room, dining room, bedroom, and separate studio. He bought furniture, decorated his walls with African masks and guitars, and even hired a maid. Despite the improved surroundings, however, Picasso's mood was dark. He often remarked that he was dying and rarely spoke except to tell Olivier he was thinking about his work. Claiming he could not paint in his new studio, he rented another one back at Bateau-Lavoir.

While his relationship with Olivier was suffering, Picasso was creating portraits that took analytical cubism to levels as yet unseen. Paintings of his three art dealers at the time, *Portrait of Vollard*, *Portrait of D.H. Kahnweiler*, and *Portrait of Wilhelm Uhde*, exemplify this evolution in style. While several of the subjects are vaguely recognizable through their facial features, the portraits are fragmented geometric shapes that look as if they are constructed from shards of broken, smoked glass. In order to give some sort of form to the painting of Kahnweiler, Picasso added elements such as his wavy hair, an earlobe, shadowed eyes, and clasped hands.

Although Kahnweiler is barely identifiable, Picasso required him to pose at thirty sittings. At first he painted a more

TRANSFIGURED, TWISTED, DEFORMED, AND HARMONIZED

In 1912, critic Josep Junoy wrote a review praising Picasso's cubist artwork, reprinted in A Picasso Anthology *edited by Marilyn McCully:*

Wherever Picasso sets his hand he leaves the imprint of his genius. . . . In no other artist have I seen so much complexity nor such an irresistibly magical strength. . . . Picasso does not paint the image reflected in his own eyes. He is not interested in representing objects . . . *photographically*, but rather in representing the idea of those objects his imagination has formed.

For Picasso representative forms of nature are not things in themselves . . . but . . . imaginary conceptions that obey the laws of the imagination —which are malleable [like clay] and therefore susceptible to being transfigured, twisted, deformed and harmonized anew.

Quoted in Marilyn McCully, *A Picasso Anthology*. Princeton, NJ: Princeton University Press, 1997, pp. 87–88.

traditional portrait, then he deconstructed it to cubism. Discussing this many years later, Picasso explained, "You must always start with something. Afterwards you can remove all trace of reality. There's no danger then. . . . Because the idea of the object will have left an indelible mark."[61]

Picasso removed another trace of reality from his life in the autumn of 1911, when he broke off his relationship with Olivier. He soon began a liaison with Marcelle Humbert, whom Picasso called Eva or Ma Jolie, after a refrain from a popular song. And, as had happened when he met Olivier in 1904, Picasso's new feelings of love brightened his mood, which was reflected in his latest work.

Collage and Constructed Sculpture

By early 1912 Picasso was adding bright yellows and purplish blues to the browns, grays, and dark blues seen in the austere analytical cubist renderings. Meanwhile, cubism had become the latest artistic sensation. Detailed books were published on the subject and dozens of young Parisian artists adopted the style. However, these practitioners, such as Marcel Duchamp, Jacques Villon, and Juan Gris, formalized a set of mathematical rules to give cubist paintings a type of order and precision that held little interest for Picasso.

Even as the cubist newcomers attracted international attention with a Paris gallery show in 1912, Picasso stayed far ahead of the competition. Others were turning cubism into abstract art, that is, the details were greatly simplified and barely alluded to the realism of the subject. Picasso, however, was bringing his work back to reality through a technique he developed called collage. In this style the artist constructed pictures from tangible, identifiable items, gluing pieces of cloth, newspaper, and other objects to the surface of his paintings.

In his new studio in Montparnasse, Picasso made *Still Life with Chair Caning* in the spring of 1912, pasting on the picture a piece of printed oilcloth that resembled woven chair caning. He also added the letters "JOU" (pun on the French word for "play") cut from the masthead of the French newspaper *Le Journal.* He then framed the entire oval picture with a piece of rope.

Another work made around this time, *Guitar*, is a cubist version of a guitar made from sheet metal and wire. In building this piece, Picasso created the first constructed sculpture. Unlike previous sculptures throughout history, *Guitar* is not cast from metal or carved from a single block of wood or stone, but rather assembled out of separate elements. This construction not only pointed a new direction for cubism, but demolished rules for sculpture that had been in place for thousands of years, opening the door for the twentieth-century constructed sculpture movement.

Guitar, made of sheet metal and wire, is representative of Picasso's work based on synthetic cubism, which brings disparate, unlikely elements together to create a single image.

Synthetic Cubism

With collage and constructed sculpture techniques, Picasso created what is now called synthetic cubism. Unlike analytic cubism, which analyzes subjects by pulling them apart into geometric pieces, synthetic cubism pushes separate pieces together into a single space. The collage *Guitar, Sheet Music and Glass* is an example of this style. To create the piece, the artist assembled a picture of a cubist guitar from seven different pieces of paper, including sheet music from a love song, wallpaper, an abstract drawing of a glass, and a piece of paper painted with wood grain to resemble a musical instrument. As Sam Hunter writes in *Picasso: Cubism and After*, these elements were meant to produce "a disrupting visual shock, since these materials had been snatched from their everyday context."[62]

During the next several years, Picasso produced dozens of vividly textured paintings based on synthetic cubism, many of them representing guitars and violins. He also produced monumental oil paintings with similar themes and content. Meanwhile, Picasso's personal life was a series of tragedies. On May 3, 1913, the artist's father, José, died in Barcelona. This caused Picasso to postpone his plans for marrying Eva who soon fell ill with a serious disease, probably breast cancer. Then Picasso's beloved dog Frika died, and the artist himself contracted a minor case of typhoid fever.

Tempering these setbacks, Picasso's works were in great demand on the French art market. One of his paintings, *Three Women*, sold for twenty thousand francs (about forty thousand dollars) in 1913. This amount, while not large by modern standards, allowed Picasso to live as a wealthy man in the Paris of the 1910s.

War and Misery

Despite Picasso's success, misery and misfortune continued to intensify with the outbreak of World War I in June 1914, followed by the German invasion of France. Tens of thousands were killed early on, and many of the artist's friends joined the army or went home to their native countries. Picasso's mood continued to blacken when Eva died in 1915.

With tanks and soldiers filling Paris streets, Picasso's artistic output slowed for the first time in his career. For example, in 1913 the artist produced nearly 350 drawings, sketches, collages, sculptures, or paintings—nearly one a day on average. By 1915, however, that number dropped to 150; in 1916, to 90. The war had also caused the bottom to drop out of the art market, and it became increasingly difficult for Picasso's dealers to sell his work. Isolated in Paris, with millions dying on nearby battlefields, Picasso's life seemed to be an unending chorus of sadness. His cubist paintings were no longer enough to send shockwaves through European society. It was time, once again, for Picasso to lead the way to a new artistic era.

Surrealistic Dreams and Nightmares

In 1916, as most of Europe was deeply embroiled in World War I, Picasso was designing theatrical sets, curtains, and costumes for a ballet called *Parade*. Written by poet, novelist, painter, and filmmaker Jean Cocteau, *Parade* centers on three groups of circus performers who hold a parade to attract an audience to their performance. Cocteau arranged for the respected Russian Ballets Russes dance troupe to perform the piece.

Parade was an experimental ballet unlike anything ever seen in the theater. The huge painting on Picasso's stage curtain was similar to his Rose Period work, filled with harlequins, winged horses, and fairy princess dancers. However, his cubist costumes with their swirls and stars were made out of solid cardboard, which severely restricted the movements of the dancers. When the production opened in Rome in 1917, audience members shouted "Dope Fiends! . . . Idiots! Scoundrels!"[63]

Although *Parade* was a critical disaster, the experience forever changed Picasso's life as well as his art. During the production he fell deeply in love with one of the Russian dancers, Olga Khoklova. The two were married in July 1918, four months before the end of World War I.

The Picasso-designed stage curtain created for the original 1917 performances of Jean Cocteau's ballet *Parade* is hung for a 2004 production in Hong Kong.

The effect of the revolutionary ballet *Parade* on the world of art was more complicated. Picasso had rewritten the script and contributed to the choreography, music, and lighting, adding extremely creative and imaginative elements to the traditional theatrics. As the troupe's set designer Léon Bakst stated: "Picasso has given us his own vision of a fairground stage, where acrobats, Chinese conjurers, and [dancers] shift around in a kaleidoscope that is simultaneously real and fantastical."[64]

Apollinaire believed Picasso's fantastic art concepts in themselves represented a new type of realism. When called upon to write the program notes for the ballet, Apollinaire called *Parade* "a kind of sur-realism [which might be] the starting point for a series of manifestations of the New Spirit that . . . promises to rearrange our arts and manners from the top to the bottom in universal happiness."[65]

"A Kind of Superior Reality"

Apollinaire died in 1918, but the term he invented, "surrealism," spawned a movement based on Picasso's art. The leading proponents of surrealism, in addition to Cocteau, were Spanish painter Joan Miró and French writers Louis Aragon and André Breton. Together they formed a new artistic group in the early 1920s called the surrealists. Their beliefs grew out of another artistic movement, Dada, founded in the wake of World War I. Dadaists, such as Marcel Duchamp, believed that the unprecedented barbarism of World War I was a result of technology, oppressive rational thought, and the values of the middle class, or bourgeoisie, whose interests drove European society and culture.

Dadaists believed that since reason, logic, and science had led to the insanity of war, the only sane reaction was to be irrational, illogical, and anarchistic. They rejected art in favor of anti-art, the most famous example of which is Duchamp's *Fountain*, a urinal displayed as artwork.

In his book *Picasso*, Patrick O'Brian explains the views held by Duchamp and others in the Dada movement: "Dadaists did not wish to preserve anything, least of all art as it was generally understood. They were disgusted with the established order; they wished to subvert it; and as far as art was concerned they meant to do away with all existing ideas, replacing the rational by irrational and divorcing thought from expression."[66] While this attitude would have described Picasso perfectly when he was in his twenties, by the end of World War I he was the supreme artist, and cubism was the "established order" that Dadaists wanted to destroy.

Breton was a Dadaist but he rejected the negativity of the movement. And as a trained psychologist, Breton was eager to see the theories of pioneering Austrian psychiatrist Sigmund Freud integrated into art. Of particular interest to Breton were Freud's theories concerning dreams, which are seen as a source of insight to unconscious desires. Breton loosely based surrealism on this concept, inspired as he was by dreamlike images that ran through his mind in the moments before falling asleep,

Picasso adopted a neoclassical style in works such as *Three Women at the Spring* at a time when Dadaists and surrealists were impacting the art world.

images that, while realistic, took place in absurd settings. The odd juxtaposition, or contrast, between reality and the incongruent, strange, and exotic forms the basis of surrealism. Breton describes this as the "fusion of elements of fantasy with elements of the modern world to form a kind of superior reality."[67]

Perhaps as a reaction to Dadaists and early surrealists, Picasso moved in the opposite direction, once again confounding his critics. Abandoning cubism, Picasso began to paint neoclassical works, a style inspired by the mythology and art of classical Greece and Rome. One of his most renowned pictures from this period is *Three Women at the Spring*, a painting of three large women that recalls ancient Greek sculpture. Picasso was likely moved to paint in this style by his visit to Rome while working on *Parade*.

Meanwhile Picasso's reputation remained intact. His work was now being shown in galleries beyond Paris, in Rome, Munich, and New York City. Publishers were also interested in the artist's work. The first book featuring his painting was published in 1921, the same year his son Paulo was born.

"Picasso's Ghoulish Humor"

In July 1925 Breton published the "Surrealist Manifesto," which he had written a year earlier. The manifesto is a rambling piece of esoteric literature that discusses Freud, dreams, culture, and the revolutionary aspects of the movement. Around the same time, Breton's magazine *La Révolution Surréaliste* published several of Picasso's paintings, including *Les Demoiselles d'Avignon*. Considered to be the original cubist painting, it was the first time *Demoiselles* was reproduced since it was created in 1907. Breton also published one of Picasso's most recent works, *Three Dancers*. This painting, the artist's first foray into surrealism, depicts three distorted figures described by Hunter:

> [In] *Three Dancers*, all the movements, distortions of form, and contrasting play of decorative areas are heightened for their more disturbing expressive possibilities. The masks of the figures are half-absurd, half-frightening. . . . Picasso's starkly patterned shapes are [fitful] in jerky angular rhythms; the movements described are the opposite of the natural articulation of the body in motion. They suggest a nervous seizure of some kind, translated into a sudden, explosive, formal activity. . . . Picasso's ghoulish humor is [demonstrated] in two ways: the rather sinister black silhouettes reinforce our fears, and the bright, garish decoration, by its very incongruity, adds a further spine tingling chill.[68]

Three Dancers represented Picasso's first surrealistic work, although he ultimately distanced himself from that movement.

Picasso allowed Breton to publish *Three Dancers* because the two men were friends. However, the artist remained aloof from the surrealists even as they adopted him as one of their own and used his work to validate their movement. For this reason, it has been said that Picasso did not join the surrealists, they joined him. Whatever the case, Wertenbaker writes that *Three Dancers* "was a harbinger of a new style in Picasso's art, [that unleashed] his inventive powers as never before."[69]

These powers of invention allowed Picasso to completely deconstruct the human form. He turned eyes sideways, twisted arms, legs, and torsos into tortured, unnatural shapes, and added shading on torsos reminiscent of his cubist collages.

AN ART MOVEMENT BASED ON A DREAM

In 1924 André Breton wrote the "Surrealist Manifesto," excerpted below, as a founding document of the movement that encompasses literature, painting, music, film, and theater. Surrealists use absurd and disjointed imagery to recreate visions like those seen in dreams, so it not surprising that the idea for surrealism is based on an image that came to Breton when he was in a dreamlike state:

One evening [as] I fell asleep, I perceived, so clearly [expressed] that it was impossible to change a word, but nonetheless removed from the sound of any voice, a rather strange phrase . . . a phrase, if I may be so bold, which was knocking at the window. . . . Actually, this phrase astonished me: unfortunately I cannot remember it exactly, but it was something like: "There is a man cut in two by the window," but there could be no question of ambiguity, accompanied as it was by the faint visual image . . . of a man walking cut half way up by a window perpendicular to the axis of his body. Beyond the slightest shadow of a doubt, what I saw was the simple reconstruction in space of a man leaning out a window. But this window having shifted with the man, I realized that I was dealing with an image of a fairly rare sort, and all I could think of was to incorporate it into my material for poetic construction.

André Breton, "Manifesto of Surrealism," Man Eating Seas, 2005. http://srrlsm.maneatingseas.com/manifesto.

Dominating, Angry Monsters

Picasso turned forty-five in 1926, and throughout the rest of the 1920s he lived the life of an internationally celebrated artist. His work was in high demand from the world's wealthiest collectors, and the money they paid for his paintings allowed him to vacation in Cannes on the French Riviera, go to the theater in Paris, and attend the most exclusive parties. While many others who had achieved such success might slow their output, Picasso remained driven, astonishing the art world with paintings that continued to push the boundaries of taste and style. And as in previous years, Picasso's art was driven by his negative emotions despite his achievements. For example, his 1929 painting *Woman in an Armchair* shows a twisted and disjointed body, dislocated eyes and breasts, an animalistic face with a gaping mouth and razor-sharp teeth, and a juxtaposition of hot and cold colors.

The surrealists, who exalted Freud, did not need a psychiatrist to understand the emotions Picasso revealed in *Woman in an Armchair*. At the time, his marriage was falling apart, and the artist was obviously portraying Olga on canvas as a dominating, angry monster whose gaping mouth and tentacle-like limbs threatened to destroy him. Picasso was also troubled by others outside his marriage. As a celebrity, Picasso was at the center of a social scene where he was treated like a modern rock star by aristocrats, artists, and others in the social elite. While he enjoyed this attention at first, Picasso soon came to resent the exaggerated praise by those Huffington calls the "tourists on the mountain peaks of creation that were his natural habitat . . . [fans] who were ready to applaud anything that came from the wizard's hand."[70]

Picasso reacted the way he always had, sleeping all day and painting all night. This did little to mend his marriage, and his dark mood was intensified by circumstances beyond his personal life. In October 1929 the stock market collapsed on Wall Street in New York, plunging the United States and Europe into a worldwide economic depression that would last throughout the 1930s. Many wealthy Americans suffered devastating financial losses, and some were forced to sell the expensive paintings they had acquired during the 1920s, depressing the price of art. In France the government cut back on funds previously available for buying art, and many successful French artists were forced to sell their work for whatever they could get. While Picasso continued to fetch high prices for his paintings, the gloom of the early Depression seemed to be reflected in his art. Many of his 1930 canvases show mangled figures and deconstructed bodies painted in monochromatic grays. Adding to Picasso's pessimism, the Nazi Party continued to consolidate power in the German government, and talk of another war was in the air. Hoping to escape the oppressive problems in Paris, Picasso bought the three-hundred-year-old, twenty-room Château de Boisgeloup near Normandy, converting the stables to studios around 1931.

A New Model

Soon after the move, the mood of Picasso's work brightened considerably, and once again the cause could be traced to a woman. Unknown to Olga, Picasso met Marie-Thérèse Walter in January 1927, when he struck up a conversation with her as she walked out of a Paris department store. Walter was tall, blond, beautiful, athletic, and earthy, and at the age of seventeen, the young German woman was less than half Picasso's age. Recalling her first meeting with the artist, Walter later said, "He simply grabbed me by the arm . . . and said, 'I'm Picasso! You and I are going to do great things together.'"[71]

Although she knew nothing about art and had never heard of Picasso, Walter agreed to meet the artist for a date. Six months later, when she turned eighteen, she became Picasso's mistress. Because he was still married to Olga, however, Picasso kept his affair secret even from his closest friends. Walter did not appear on canvas until 1932 when Picasso placed her in a series of paintings that signaled a move away from his biting, angry portrayals of Olga.

At Boisgeloup, isolated from art dealers, reporters, fans, friends, and family, Picasso poured his creative energies into paintings that expressed his feelings for Walter. In most of these, she is portrayed in repose, in an armchair, or with a mirror. Her skin is rendered in pastel purples and pinks, her limbs and wavy hair flow like water, her posture languid and peaceful. Picasso's favorite from this era, *Girl Before a Mirror*, is painted with vivid reds, oranges, purples, and greens. The imagery in the painting is described by Enrique Mallen, director of the On-Line Picasso Project:

> This particular mirror—psyché in French—symbolically reveals the inner self, but also relates to vanity, the appearance of the exterior. The face of the physical self on the left possesses many familiar characteristics of Marie-Thérèse. The coloring of its two sides, however, differs drastically; the violet half has been interpreted as Marie-Thérèse's calm exterior, while the brilliant yellow and red of the other side may represent her more ardent desires. The stripes on the figure's "real" and reflected torsos add another symbolic layer if they are read as ribs, or a skeleton . . . they may also be a coded reference to Picasso himself.[72]

Picasso's young German mistress, Marie-Thérèse Walter, was the subject of a series of paintings that included *Girl before a Mirror.*

Picasso's portraits of Walter were scheduled to be shown in the artist's first retrospective exhibition at the Galérie Georges Petit in the summer of 1932. Picasso would also be showing over two hundred other pictures from the past thirty years, including portraits of Casagemas in his coffin and major works from the Blue, Rose, and cubist periods. (Although many of these paintings belonged to collectors, they were loaned back to the artist for the exhibition.) Picasso threw himself into making the exhibition perfect, hanging the pictures himself and overseeing the lighting. He even planned to attend the opening, something he had rarely done at previous shows. Commenting on the importance of this event, O'Brian writes, "Hitherto Paris had seen Picasso in bits and pieces; and although he was now fifty, his reputation . . . was founded more on talk, partial information, and general notoriety than on a firm, widely-based appreciation."[73]

When the exhibition opened in July, some of the most respected artists, writers, and composers of the day were in attendance, and critics agreed Picasso was the most important artist of the twentieth century. However, the show was also the first time that Olga saw the portraits of Walter and understood that her husband was having an affair.

Picasso's *Minotauromachy*, with its violent surrealistic imagery, is the most revered painting from the artist's Minotaur Period.

The Minotaur Period

Perhaps because of the poisonous atmosphere of his domestic situation, possibly because Adolph Hitler was elected chancellor of Germany, Picasso's subject matter shifted once again in 1933 as he entered what is known as his Minotaur Period. In

February the Nazis created huge public spectacles, burning books in the streets. They also opened the first concentration camp at Dachau and filled it with Jews, Communists, and labor leaders. In France the surrealists began searching for a new symbol to represent the atrocious events. They settled on the minotaur—a half-bull, half-man monster from Greek mythology—to represent mankind's bestial and violent nature.

On May 25 the surrealist magazine *Minotaure* began publication, the cover featuring a reproduction of a surrealistic minotaur by Picasso. In the several following years the minotaur, along with Walter, would be a recurring theme for Picasso, but the artist modified the imagery of the beast, showing it as a sightless, vulnerable monster that could either interact with people peacefully or commit senseless violence. Oftentimes, this creature represents the artist and his relationship to women, especially in works such as *Blind Minotaur Guided Through a Starry Night by Marie-Thérèse with a Pigeon.*

Picasso's most revered painting of the period, *Minotauromachy*, depicts a bull-headed minotaur, representing the artist, stopped in its tracks by a young girl holding a candle after the beast has violently gored a horse. The painting is critical of both the artist and his female companions, a commentary on Picasso's belief that men use their strength to have their way and women use their charms to conquer men. Created during a period the artist called "the worst time in my life,"[74] the female picador with the swollen belly in the painting is clearly Walter who, in reality, had unexpectedly become pregnant.

The scene in *Minotauromachy* is as chaotic and complicated as Picasso's personal life at the time. Walter's pregnancy prompted Olga to move to the south of France with Picasso's son Paulo. Walter gave birth to Maria de la Concepcion Picasso, known as Maya, in September 1935. However, Picasso remained unwilling to grant Olga a divorce because he refused to divide his property with her. They lived apart but remained married until Olga died in 1955. Meanwhile, Picasso had taken another mistress, twenty-nine-year-old Dora Maar, a respected photographer and painter in her own right. As with his

The Los Angeles County Museum of Art Web site "Picasso's Greatest Print: The Minotauromachy in All Its States," describes the symbolism of the masterpiece Minotauromachy:

Silhouetted against sea and sky, a bull-headed Minotaur (Picasso's alter ego throughout the 1930s) advances with one arm outstretched toward a young girl (sometimes identified as Marie-Thérèse), who, calm in the face of his approach, stands holding a lit candle in one hand and a bouquet of flowers in the other. The Minotaur, whose gesture and demeanor are traditionally interpreted as threatening, appears to shield himself from the light cast by the candle. Between girl and beast, a terrified horse rears on its hind legs in panic; entrails ooze from a gash in its belly (presumably caused by the Minotaur). Collapsed across the horse's back, a half-naked, unconscious female matador (possibly pregnant and unmistakably bearing the facial features of Marie-Thérèse) holds a sword poised between Minotaur and horse. On the far left, a bearded man (who may also represent Picasso), observes this scene from a ladder propped against a wall, while two young women with two doves watch impassively from a window in a plain stone building. . . . [Through] the use of highly personal themes and motifs, Picasso forged a multilayered, universal allegory of good and evil, violence and innocence, suffering and salvation.

Los Angeles County Museum of Art, "Picasso's Greatest Print: The Minotauromachy in All Its States," 2006. www.lacma.org/art/PicassoIndex.aspx.

other loves, Picasso soon began immortalizing Maar on canvas. One of those paintings, *Dora Maar with Cat* sold for $95.2 million in 2006, making it the world's second most expensive painting ever sold at auction.

Guernica

Maar appeared in Picasso's life as he was tapping the violent surrealistic imagery of *Minotauromachy* for what is perhaps his most famous painting, *Guernica*. The genesis of the mural dates to April 26, 1937, when German Nazi planes flew over the little medieval Spanish town of Guernica. The citizens there opposed Spain's fascist military leader, Francisco Franco, during the Spanish civil war, which was raging at the time. At 4:40 in the afternoon the Nazis dropped incendiary bombs on civilians, machine-gunning those who ran. The ancient village was reduced to rubble, and 1,645 of its 7,000 civilians were killed and nearly 900 wounded. This was a new type of attack, only the second time in history that innocent civilians in a defenseless town were bombed from the air. The first bombing, in the rural town of Durango, had passed largely unnoticed when it occurred several weeks earlier. However, the Guernica attack was soon made famous by Picasso, who had been commissioned to paint a mural for the Spanish pavilion in the 1937 Paris World's Fair.

The horror and violence of a Nazi aerial bombing of a Spanish town inspired Picasso to create *Guernica* for exhibition at the 1937 World's Fair in Paris.

Picasso began by making forty-five sketches, all of which were meticulously documented in photographs taken by Maar. Picasso then transferred the imagery to a huge canvas, 12 feet high (3.6m) and 26 feet across (8m). In somber tones of black, dirty white, and deep gray Picasso painted surrealistic figures emitting silent screams among chaos and carnage. Discussing the meaning of *Guernica*, Picasso stated: "In the picture . . . I clearly express my loathing for the military caste that has plunged Spain into a sea of suffering and death."[75]

When *Guernica* was exhibited, the painting elicited admiration and excitement along with hatred and protest from Franco's supporters. Two years later the Nazis invaded Poland, initiating World War II. By the time the war ended in 1945, millions of innocent civilians had been killed on both sides by bombs dropped from airplanes. Aerial bombing was now an acceptable military practice. However, historians continue to view *Guernica* as one of the greatest antiwar statements ever put on canvas. For the fifty-five-year-old Picasso, it was one of hundreds of paintings that encapsulated raw emotional feelings that were both personal for the artist and universal for those who viewed his work.

The Move to Neo-Expressionism

On June 14, 1940, on one of the bleakest days of World War II, the Nazis marched into Paris and began a totalitarian occupation that lasted four and a half years. The Nazi occupation was a time of excessive hardship for the people of France. Jewish people, intellectuals, professors, homosexuals, and artists were deported to concentration camps to die. While thousands were attempting to flee France, Picasso chose to remain in his Paris studio despite several offers to help him emigrate to the United States or Mexico.

By this time Picasso was a very wealthy man, and this undoubtedly helped him deal with the occupation. However, Hitler had labeled Picasso's paintings "degenerate art," a term used by the Nazis to describe almost all modern art, which was deemed un-German or pro-Jewish. Degenerate artists were forbidden from exhibiting, selling, or even producing their work. Describing this period in *Picasso and the War Years*, Stephen Nash writes:

> Picasso lived under the oppressive weight of German surveillance, manifested most blatantly by occasional searches of his studio by Nazi soldiers. . . . It is clear

that Picasso's financial well being allowed for privileges that eased the discomfort of life made grim by Occupation shortages, and his status as a famous artist respected around the world brought from certain quarters a favoritism that . . . helped on occasion to keep him safe. In general, however, he sought to . . . remain invisible.[76]

While remaining out of public sight, Picasso continued to create, basing his work on themes that reflected his situation during the war. In addition to painting radiators, candles, and food, representing wartime shortages of heat, electricity, and provisions, Picasso painted odd portraits. These are described by Michael Kimmelman in the *New York Times* as "abstracted faces twisted like slabs of hard, flat rubber into knots or made to look like blocks of jagged crystal. The expressions . . . tend to be wide-eyed but impassive. These are mute monsters, occupying confined, hermetic spaces. Figure and room are often knitted together by an obsessive tangle of spiky lines."[77]

A Dirty Brush for Dirty Deeds

When the Germans were finally driven out of Paris in 1944, Picasso was sixty-three years old. It had been more than forty-five years since he embarked on his career as an artist and thirty-seven since his first experiments with cubism. During those years, Picasso had influenced artists across the globe, and now that the war was over the artist was more popular than ever. As Wertenbaker writes, "In seemed in the fall of 1944 as if Picasso loved everybody and everybody loved him. . . . Most Parisians agreed that he was the most popular figure in liberated France. . . . [The] only person who compared with him . . . was the war hero General Charles de Gaulle."[78]

Just weeks after the liberation, Picasso joined the French Communist Party and worked with its members to host an exhibition of his paintings at the renowned Salon d'Automne. It was the first art exhibit since the occupation began and was jubilantly called the Liberation Salon. Picasso chose about seventy paintings for the exhibit, all done since 1940 and none seen by the public. Controversy quickly erupted, however, since it was the first time a foreigner had been allowed to take over the entire hall of this important gallery for a one-person show. Two days after the exhibit opened, a mob of right-wing students rushed the gallery and tore Picasso's paintings from the wall, protesting Picasso's rev-

Inspired by gruesome images of Nazi concentration camps, Picasso's *Charnel House* depicts the victims of wartime atrocities.

olutionary art and Communist beliefs. Art critics had other problems with the paintings. British reviewer Michael Ayrton wrote that Picasso was simply repeating themes he had long relied on, only with less creativity: "His pictures are uniformly dung colored. . . . He is now engaged in the intellectual activity of flogging his own clichés to death with one dirty brush."[79]

While other critics defended the show, Picasso, as always, ignored the press and continued to express himself. By the spring of 1945, the Allied armies had pushed into Germany, liberating the first concentration camps where millions had been slaughtered. When the depravities of the Holocaust first appeared in news photos, Picasso once again stretched a huge canvas to commemorate victims of wartime atrocities in *Charnel House*. Like *Guernica*, the painting is monochromatic, in black, grey, and white. But the surrealistic figures are not screaming in terror as in *Guernica*, but dead, their twisted, desiccated corpses tied into knots.

"Without Tears"

According to Nash, Picasso considered *Charnel House* and *Guernica* as "pendants that together would stand as bracketing statements around the wartime period."[80] As his anger from the war subsided, Picasso once again felt elation when he found a new lover, twenty-one-year-old Françoise Gilot, a painter whom he had arranged to meet after viewing her work in a small gallery in Paris. Like his previous girlfriends, Gilot soon became the focus of Picasso's artwork and appeared in dozens of portraits, sometimes in the form of a flower with leaves for hair and petals for breasts. Within a year of their meeting, Gilot gave birth to a boy, Claude. In 1949 the couple would have a second child, a daughter Paloma.

By the time of Paloma's birth, Picasso had settled with his new family in the town of Vallauris in southern France. The region was known for its soil, which was excellent for making pottery, and during this period Picasso set aside his canvases for lumps of local clay. Picasso called his ceramics "sculpture without tears,"[81] because the fired clay objects were small and easy to handle, and he was soon creating hundreds of ceramic designs with bulls, birds, and female figures. He also made everyday objects, such as casserole dishes and plates, and painted them with lively designs of bullfights. In this manner, Picasso produced over two thousand pieces of clay and ceramic sculpture.

Pregnant Woman was one of more than two thousand clay and ceramic works Picasso created after settling in Vallauris, France.

Politics and Art

While ceramics satisfied Picasso's artistic side, for the first time in his life he became overtly political, devoting his time to the Communists. He took his first airplane ride when he gave a speech at the World Peace Congress held in Wroclaw, Poland, in 1948. Soon after, the artist became a leading figure in the Communist-led peace movement, readily used by the Soviets who realized the propaganda value of having such a celebrity in their ranks. However, this harmed Picasso's reputation in the West, especially in the United States where communism was reviled by many who associated it with totalitarian Soviet dictator Joseph Stalin. Picasso caused further controversy when he donated a drawing of a Milanese pigeon with a beautiful

PICASSO AND COMMUNISM

Communism is based on the political philosophy that a nation's property and wealth belong to all members of society, and everyone is equal, from factory workers to artists and national leaders. During World War II, the Communist Soviet Union joined France and the United States against Germany. After the war the Communists were respected in France for their resistance against the Nazis. When Picasso joined the French Communist Party immediately after the war, he did so based on his belief in equality and social justice. However, communism came to be one of the most hated and divisive political theories of the twentieth century, especially after the Soviet Union imposed a totalitarian government on all of Eastern Europe in the postwar years.

Because of his Communist beliefs Picasso was widely criticized in the United States and other Western countries. When Picasso applied for a visa to the United States to attend a world peace conference in 1950, he was denied permission to enter the country. The FBI refused to allow the artist into the country because he was a Communist. Picasso finally quit the Communist Party in the mid-1950s, around the time the world learned that Soviet dictator Joseph Stalin had killed more of his own people than Hitler had. Before that, however, much of Picasso's postwar art was influenced by his political beliefs.

frilly neck and long white feathers for use by Louis Aragon, a leader in the French Communist Party. Aragon used the picture to promote the World Congress for the Partisans of Peace. Cabanne describes how this simple work of art quickly became an international symbol of peace:

> Aragon took one look at the pigeon: pigeon to dove, dove to peace . . . and thus was born the Dove of Peace,

henceforth destined to circle the world. It was almost noon; Aragon rushed to the printer's with the print. A few hours later, *The Dove of Peace* was coming off the presses. . . . To [Picasso's] great delight his Party comrades would bring the [poster] to a worldwide audience.[82]

Posters of the dove appeared within hours on walls and buildings all over Paris, and in the months that followed, Picasso continued to rework the symbol. Since that time Picasso's dove motif has been reproduced countless times, and since the 1960s his doves have appeared on posters, coffee mugs, bumper stickers, T-shirts, and even postage stamps in China and the Soviet Union. In the early fifties, however, Picasso's association with the Communists caused his sales to drop and the value of his paintings to fall worldwide. In addition, he was widely derided in the press. *ARTnews* attacked Picasso as a "staunch poster-designer and part-time propagandist," while the *New York Times* mocked his "fat little pigeons."[83]

While alienating many of his former supporters, nonpartisan critics also believe that Picasso's art in the postwar years suffered as a result of his political leanings. As art historian Gertje Utley writes in *ARTnews*:

> For students of Picasso, the decade right after World War II has often been considered less interesting. . . . People generally look at his paintings first, and that period, simply in terms of painting, isn't that exciting. . . . It was precisely the period of his most active commitment to the Communist Party. Quite a bit of time went into traveling for the party and filling the constant demands placed on him. And when you see the variety of his creative work at the time—ceramics, lithographs, and party posters—it fits very well with his political preoccupations.[84]

Picasso's support of communism began to wane in the early 1950s because the Soviets found much to criticize in his artistic style. In fact, they sounded little different from his Western critics. One reviewer writing for a Moscow magazine stated "His works . . . provoke the indignation of the simple people. . . . His every canvas deforms man, his body, his face."[85] Tensions were further inflamed by Picasso's cartoonlike sketch of Soviet leader Joseph Stalin as a young man. When the portrait was published in a Communist weekly on the occasion of Stalin's death in 1953, the Communists thought Picasso was making fun of their revered leader and criticized him severely. After the flare-up, when asked why he had joined the Communist Party in the first place, Picasso said, "I thought it would be a big, brotherly family . . . now I hate my family!"[86]

Although Picasso's reputation suffered because of his political views, his *Dove of Peace* became a popular antiwar symbol.

The Human Comedy

Picasso had more on his mind than Stalin in the summer of 1953 when Gilot broke off her relations with him, moving to Paris with the children. She later said she began to see Picasso, now over seventy, as an old man for the first time. Picasso took the break hard, and his work reflected the feelings of a heartbroken and bitter man. In the months that followed, he produced a series of 180 drawings with a "painter and model" theme that the artist called a visual diary. In many of the drawings, the model is a beautiful young woman, obviously Gilot, and the person painting her, obviously Picasso, is represented alternately as a diminutive clown, a monkey, a leering old man, or an insignificant figure barely in the frame. Many of the drawings are made with the barest of outlines in bright colors made with crayons, as if sketched by a child. When the drawings were published in 1954 under the title *Picasso and the Human Comedy*, most critics did not appreciate the turmoil under which the pictures were created, judging them simply by their outward appearance. However, critic Michel Leiris aptly describes them as a "visual journal of a detestable season in hell,

Picasso, center in white shirt, and his then-girlfriend Jacqueline Roque, to the left of Picasso, attend a bullfight in 1955. Jacqueline became the inspiration behind many of Picasso's works during their years as a couple.

a crisis of his inner life which led him on to the widest kind of questioning."[87]

By now it had become a cliché that Picasso's paintings changed whenever he met a new woman. However, that is exactly what happened when he took up with twenty-seven-year-old Jacqueline Roque, a petite divorcee who worked at Madoura Pottery where Picasso made ceramics. Roque moved in with Picasso in 1954 and became his second wife in 1961, when the artist was seventy-nine. During the early years of their relationship, Picasso created more works of art based on Roque than any of his other loves, including seventy portraits of her in a single year. Unlike the sometimes cruel paintings of his previous partners, Picasso was more complimentary to Roque, according to journalist Sandra Kwock-Silve: "Although there is an ongoing sense of experimentation with form and line, neither are ever jarring, or unflattering as in the portraits of Dora Maar, or the cold, analytical depictions of Marie Thérèse Walter."[88]

Roque was fiercely protective of Picasso and, as the artist became more reclusive during their relationship, she screened all but the most important visitors. Old friends and even his children Claude and Paloma were denied entry into his new mansion, called La Californie, near Cannes.

Reworking the Masters

In the process of immortalizing Roque on canvas, Picasso turned to a type of art that few professional artists have ever attempted. According to Marie-Laure Bernadac in *Late Picasso*, the artist:

ceaselessly analyzed, decomposed, and recomposed other men's masterpieces, digesting them to make them his own. This pictorial cannibalism is unprecedented in the history of art.... From one painting he makes a hundred, feverishly exploring all the possibilities on offer in the endeavor to validate his own handiwork, to test the power of his painting on [any] given subject matter.[89]

Picasso's first work in the series, *Women of Algiers*, completed in 1955, was originally painted in 1834 by French romantic master Eugène Delacroix. The painting of women in a harem had preoccupied Picasso for years, and he often visited the Louvre to view it when he needed inspiration. Now, it intrigued Picasso that one of the languid women in Delacroix's painting strongly resembled Roque. For a three-month period, the artist obsessively deconstructed *Women of Algiers* into a series of nearly one hundred sketches and fifteen oil paintings. One of the final pieces, *The Women of Algiers (Version "O")*, is a colorful cubist masterpiece described by Bernadac:

Picasso's take on Eugène Delacroix's *Women of Algiers* was the first in a series of paintings in which he recreated other artists' masterpieces in his own style.

Picasso enters into the game with huge gusto, giving rein to a joyously aggressive eroticism far removed from the cushioned sensuousness of the harem. He kneads the springy flesh, bends it with his agile brush into twists and arabesques, then slams it into a rigorous geometric pattern of acute angles and faceted volumes that has its origin in Cubism. . . . [He] transforms the composition into his favorite theme of a seated female figure watching over a sleeping one.[90]

Picasso then embarked on a journey into seventeenth-century Spain, creating several variations on the canvas *Las Meniñas*, painted in 1656 by Spanish master Diego Velásquez. The original depicts a Spanish king, queen, princess, and ladies-in-waiting being painted by Velásquez himself, the back of his canvas occupying a prominent place on the left side of the picture. Because it featured Picasso's favorite theme of artist and model, the painting was ripe for reinterpretation. Picasso spent two months producing forty-four versions of *Las Meniñas* with cubist geometry and overlapping planes. Some are comic parodies of the painting while others are serious interpretations in a unique style.

A New Expression in Art

Picasso continued reworking the masters until 1963. Paintings produced during this period include Picasso's versions of Manet's 1863 *Luncheon on the Grass* and Jacques-Louis David's 1799 *The Rape of the Sabines*. After nearly eight years of deconstructing the masters, Picasso turned to printmaking, the process of making prints on paper using techniques such as engraving and etching.

An engraving is made when an artist draws a design directly on a metal plate using a sharp metal cutting device called a burin. The metal plate is placed on a printing press, allowing the artist to make multiple copies. In etching, a metal plate is covered with an acid-resistant varnish, and the artist scratches off the varnish with an etching needle, exposing the metal below. This is immersed in an acid bath which eats away the ex-

PICASSO'S NEO-EXPRESSIONISM

During the last years of his life, Picasso's studio was filled with etchings and paintings that critics dismissed as childish or perverse. It was only after his 1973 death that critics were able to identify and understand the neo-Expressionism in Picasso's work, a technique he invented which dominated the art market in the 1980s. An article on the World Wide Art Resources Web site describes neo-Expressionism:

*A*lthough the Neo-Expressionists tended to draw their influence from many sources, the late aggressive paintings of Pablo Picasso were a major inspiration. . . . Neo-Expressionist paintings were characterized by a rough, violent approach and the return to more conventional formats such as easel paintings. Quite often, Neo-Expressionist works contained the human figure. . . . Neo-Expressionist paintings were normally large and created quickly, occasionally incorporating found objects. Other tenets of the movement included slashing brushstrokes, strong color contrasts, and distorted subject matter. Neo-Expressionist paintings were more concerned with displaying spontaneous emotion rather than traditional conventions.

World Wide Art Resources, "Neo-Expressionism," February 5, 2006. wwar.com/masters/movements/neo_expressionism.html.

posed metal. After the plate is cleaned and inked, it is placed on a press to make copies. Picasso also used variations of these processes called drypoint and aquatint.

Many of Picasso's prints and oil paintings made between 1965 and 1971 are filled with often roughly detailed phalluses, breasts, and human bodies intertwined in love. According to Belgian art critic Bruno Dillen on the Art in the Picture Web site, "these works were dismissed by most as pornographic fantasies of an impotent old man, or the slapdash works of an artist who was past

Late in his career, Picasso took up printmaking, creating etchings such as *Ecce Homo*.

his prime."[91] Another critic, Douglas Cooper, called Picasso's later creations "the incoherent scribblings of a frenetic old man in the antechamber of death."[92] However, in the 1970s, after Picasso's death, critics began analyzing these prints and paintings, only to discover that the artist had invented neo-Expressionism. This is a style of modern painting where the human body is recognizable but portrayed in violent, emotional ways with vivid, garish colors. Once again Picasso was ahead of his time.

Chicago Picasso

While living the life of a recluse and making neo-Expressionist paintings in southern France, Picasso designed what is undoubtedly his most public work, one that is viewed by tens of thousands of people every day. In 1965 Picasso was contacted by William Hartmann, the chief architect of the Daley Center, a steel-and-glass, thirty-one-story skyscraper in downtown Chicago. Hartmann wanted Picasso to create a public sculpture for Daley Plaza located in front of the building. While few imagined that the artist would comply with such a request for a city he never saw in a country he never visited, Picasso quickly created a 42-inch steel model (107cm) of a creature somewhat resembling a giant bird or a winged horse. The

The steel sculpture by Picasso that stands in Chicago's Daley Plaza has become a landmark attraction for the city.

model was turned into a sculpture 50 feet high (15.2m), weighing 162 tons (146mt), built from the same type of steel used on the skyscraper. Three charitable foundations came forward to pay for the fabrication of the sculpture. Picasso turned down the one-hundred-thousand-dollar fee he was offered, preferring to present the design and the model as a "gift to the people of Chicago."[93] (This was a diplomatic gesture on the part of the artist—the market value of the work was far beyond the funds available.) Since it was unveiled in 1967, the sculpture known as *Chicago Picasso* has become one of the most recognizable landmarks in the city.

Waking Up the Mind

Picasso died suddenly of heart failure on April 8, 1973. Until that day, the ninety-one-year-old artist continued to work as he always had, rising at noon and often creating artwork until six o'clock in the morning. When he died, he left dozens of sketches, drawings, and unfinished paintings for works he was planning for the coming year. By this time, Picasso's impact on generations of artists was well documented. In the United States, some of the world's best-known artists, including Willem de Kooning, Jasper Johns, Roy Lichtenstein, Jackson Pollock, and Max Weber "directly and openly interpreted Picasso's style, appropriated his palette, or used his work as a point of departure,"[94] according to the San Francisco Museum of Modern Art Web site. From cubism to surrealism to neo-Expressionism, Picasso created more masterpieces in a year than many create in a lifetime. For more than seventy-five years, the artistic mastermind from Málaga portrayed joy, depression, love, hatred, and the human drama while creating a new way for people to see the world. Commenting on his contribution, Picasso declared, "[For] me painting is a dramatic action in the course of which reality finds itself split apart. . . . What interests me is to set up the most unexpected relationship possible between things. . . . I want to draw the mind in a direction it's not used to and wake it up."[95]

Notes

Introduction: A Creative Force of Nature

1. Marina Picasso, *Picasso: My Grandfather*. New York: Riverhead, 2001, p. 4.
2. Quoted in Arianna Huffington, *Picasso: Creator and Destroyer*. New York: Simon & Schuster, 1988, p. 10.
3. Quoted in Barcelona Apartments, "Picasso," 2005. **http://rentalona.com/barcelona/pablo-picasso.htm.**

Chapter 1: A Young Artist

4. Norman Mailer, *Portrait of Picasso as a Young Man*. New York: Atlantic Monthly, 1995, p. 3.
5. Quoted in Lael Wertenbaker, *The World of Picasso*. Alexandria, VA: Time-Life, 1967, p. 9.
6. Quoted in Jaime Sabartés, *Picasso: An Intimate Portrait*. New York: Prentice, 1948, p. 39.
7. Wertenbaker, *The World of Picasso*, pp. 11–12.
8. Quoted in Wertenbaker, *The World of Picasso*, p. 11.
9. Wertenbaker, *The World of Picasso*, p. 11.
10. Quoted in Marilyn McCully, ed., *Picasso: The Early Years, 1892–1906.* Washington, DC: National Gallery of Art, 1997, p. 23.
11. Huffington, *Picasso: Creator and Destroyer*, p. 39.
12. Huffington, *Picasso: Creator and Destroyer*, pp. 32–33.
13. Mailer, *Portrait of Picasso as a Young Man*, p. 13.
14. McCully, *Picasso: The Early Years, 1892–1906*, p. 26.
15. Quoted in Mailer, *Portrait of Picasso as a Young Man*, p. 17.
16. Picasso Museum, "Museu Picasso," 2007. **www.museupicasso.bcn.es/eng/index_eng.htm.**
17. Quoted in Huffington, *Picasso: Creator and Destroyer*, p. 41.

Chapter 2: Sadness, Pain, and the Blue Period

18. Quoted in John Richardson, *A Life of Picasso, Volume 1: 1881–1906.* New York: Random House, 1991, p. 113.
19. Sabartés, *Picasso: An Intimate Portrait*, p. 52.
20. Quoted in Marilyn McCully, *Els Quatre Gats: Art in Barcelona Around 1900*. Princeton, NJ: Princeton University Art Museum/Princeton University Press, 1978, p. 18.

21. Sabartés, *Picasso: An Intimate Portrait*, p. 52.
22. Quoted in Marilyn McCully, *A Picasso Anthology*. Princeton, NJ: Princeton University Press, 1997, p. 23.
23. Quoted in McCully, *A Picasso Anthology*, p. 23.
24. Quoted in McCully, *A Picasso Anthology*, p. 24.
25. Pierre Cabanne, *Pablo Picasso: His Life and Times*. New York: William Morrow, 1977, p. 54.
26. Cabanne, *Pablo Picasso: His Life and Times*, p. 54.
27. Cabanne, *Pablo Picasso: His Life and Times*, pp. 55–56.
28. Quoted in Cabanne, *Pablo Picasso: His Life and Times*, p. 56.
29. Huffington, *Picasso: Creator and Destroyer*, p. 55.
30. Quoted in McCully, *A Picasso Anthology*, p. 33.
31. Sabartés, *Picasso: An Intimate Portrait*, p. 65.
32. Quoted in McCully, *Picasso: The Early Years, 1892–1906*, p. 39.
33. Wertenbaker, *The World of Picasso*, p. 44.

Chapter 3: Love and Roses
34. Cabanne, *Pablo Picasso: His Life and Times*, p. 90.
35. Fernande Olivier, *Loving Picasso*. New York: Henry N. Abrams, 2001, p. 139.
36. Mailer, *Portrait of Picasso as a Young Man*, p. 93.
37. Olivier, *Loving Picasso*, p. 140.
38. Olivier, *Loving Picasso*, p. 157.
39. Quoted in Joseph Palau i Fabre, *Picasso: The Early Years, 1881–1907*. New York: Konemann, 1981, p. 428.
40. Cabanne, *Pablo Picasso: His Life and Times*, p. 119.
41. Richardson, *A Life of Picasso*, p. 405.
42. Quoted in Mailer, *Portrait of Picasso as a Young Man*, p. 214.
43. Olivier, *Loving Picasso*, p. 182.
44. Quoted in McCully, *Picasso: The Early Years, 1892–1906*, p. 277.
45. Richardson, *A Life of Picasso*, p. 428.
46. Quoted in Huffington, *Picasso: Creator and Destroyer*, p. 90.

Chapter 4: Creating Cubism
47. Cabanne, *Pablo Picasso: His Life and Times*, p. 113.
48. Quoted in André Malraux, *Picasso's Mask*. New York: Holt, Rinehart and Winston, 1976, pp. 10–11.
49. Thomas Hoving, "Nothing Like It," *Los Angeles Times*, May 8, 2007, p. A23.
50. Quoted in Leland de la Durantaye, "Never Mind Euclid, Here's the Cubists," *Boston Globe*, December 25, 2006, p. K5.
51. Quoted in de la Durantaye, "Never Mind Euclid, Here's the Cubists," p. K5.
52. Quoted in Jonathan Jones, "Fragments of the Universe," *Guardian*, May 22, 2004. http://arts.guardian.co.uk/features/story/0,11710,1222 057,00.html.

53. Quoted in Wertenbaker, *The World of Picasso*, p. 54.

54. Quoted in Cabanne, *Pablo Picasso: His Life and Times*, p. 119.

55. Quoted in Cabanne, *Pablo Picasso: His Life and Times*, p. 119.

56. Wertenbaker, *The World of Picasso*, p. 55.

57. Richardson, *A Life of Picasso*, p. 474.

58. Quoted in Wertenbaker, *The World of Picasso*, p. 57.

59. John Golding, "Cubism, a History and an Analysis, 1907–1914," Mark Harden's Artchive, 2000. www.art chive.com/artchive/P/picasso/hort ebro.jpg.html.

60. Wertenbaker, *The World of Picasso*, pp. 57–58.

61. Quoted in John Richardson, *A Life of Picasso, Volume 2: 1907–1917*. New York: Random House, 1996, p. 175.

62. Sam Hunter, *Picasso: Cubism and After*. New York: Harry N. Abrams, 1969, p. 12.

Chapter 5: Surrealistic Dreams and Nightmares

63. Quoted in Cabanne, *Pablo Picasso: His Life and Times*, p. 188.

64. Quoted in Anne Baldassari, ed., *The Surrealist Picasso*. Riehen/Basel: Fondation Beyeler, 2005, p. 10.

65. Quoted in Cabanne, *Pablo Picasso: His Life and Times*, p. 189.

66. Patrick O'Brian, *Picasso*. New York: G.P. Putnam's Sons, 1976, p. 263.

67. Quoted in Art History Archive, "The Origins of Surrealism," 2007. www.arthistoryarchive.com/arthis tory/surrealism/Origins-of-Surreal ism.html.

68. Hunter, *Picasso: Cubism and After*, p. 18.

69. Wertenbaker, *The World of Picasso*, p. 83.

70. Huffington, *Picasso: Creator and Destroyer*, p. 192.

71. Quoted in Huffington, *Picasso: Creator and Destroyer*, p. 188.

72. Enrique Mallen, "On-Line Picasso Project," Texas A&M University, 2007. http://picasso.tamu.edu/pic asso.

73. O'Brian, *Picasso*, p. 291.

74. Quoted in Los Angeles County Museum of Art, "Picasso's Greatest Print: The Minotauromachy in All Its States," 2006. www.lacma.org/ art/PicassoIndex.aspx.

75. Quoted in O'Brian, *Picasso*, p. 321.

Chapter 6: The Move to Neo-Expressionism

76. Stephen Nash, ed., *Picasso and the War Years*. New York: Thames and Hudson, 1999, p. 25.

77. Michael Kimmelman, "Occupied Paris and the Politics of Picasso," *New York Times*, February 5, 1999. http://query.nytimes.com/gst/full page.html?res=9C00E5DF1F38F9 36A35751C0A96F958260&sec= &spon=&pagewanted=2.

78. Wertenbaker, *The World of Picasso*, p. 145.

79. Quoted in Nash, *Picasso and the War Years*, p. 29.

80. Nash, *Picasso and the War Years*, p. 35.

81. Quoted in Wertenbaker, *The World of Picasso*, p. 149.

82. Cabanne, *Pablo Picasso: His Life and Times*, p. 407.

83. Quoted in Hugh Eakin, "Picasso's Party Line," ARTnews, November 2000. http://artnews.com/issues/article.asp?art_id=809.

84. Quoted in Eakin, "Picasso's Party Line."

85. Quoted in Wertenbaker, *The World of Picasso*, p. 149.

86. Quoted in Wertenbaker, *The World of Picasso*, p. 151.

87. Quoted in "Picasso, La Comedie Humaine," Hornseys, 2007. http://hornseys.com/artist/picasso—la-comedie-humaine.

88. Sandra Kwock-Silve, "'Intimate Picasso' Opens New Art Museum," *Paris Voice*, March 2004. www.parisvoice.com/voicearchives/03/dec/html/art/art.html.

89. Quoted in Pablo Picasso, *Late Picasso: Paintings, Sculpture, Drawings, Prints, 1953–1972*. London: Tate Gallery, 1988, p. 54.

90. Quoted in Picasso, *Late Picasso*, p. 56.

91. Bruno Dillen, "Biography," Art in the Picture, 2005. http://artinthepiture.com/artists/Pablo_Picasso/biography.html.

92. Quoted in Dillen, "Biography," Art in the Picture.

93. Quoted in Chicago Public Library, "1967 August 15—Picasso Statue Unveiled in Civic Center Plaza," August 1997. www.chipublib.org/004chicago/timeline/picasso.html.

94. San Francisco Museum of Modern Art, "Picasso and American Art," 2007. www.sfmoma.org.

95. Quoted in Art Gallery New South Wales, "Picasso: The Last Decades," 2007. www.artgallery.nsw.gov.au/picasso.

Glossary

anarchy: A political theory that rejects government authority and believes that society is better served through cooperation of individuals and groups.

aquatint: A method of etching in a copper plate that produces prints that resemble watercolor paintings.

art nouveau: French for "new art," a highly decorative style of art, architecture, and furniture design that was popular in the 1890s, characterized by flowing curved lines and ornamental flower or plant patterns.

burin: A sharp metal cutting tool used to draw designs directly on a metal plate during the engraving process.

cubism: An artistic style pioneered by Picasso that represented natural forms as geometric shapes seen from several different angles at once.

curvilinear: A form characterized by curved lines.

drypoint: A technique of engraving on copper with a sharp-pointed needle that produces a print with soft, velvety lines.

esoteric: Something difficult to understand or understood by only a few select people.

harlequin: A clown-like, comic character who is agile and acrobatic. Also a character of myth and legend who plays jokes on people and disobeys the normal conventions of society.

impressionist: An artist who paints in the style of impressionism, using bright, unmixed colors to create pictures that give a simplified impression, rather than a realistic view of a subject.

modernism: A style of art that developed in the late nineteenth century characterized as a rejection of painting techniques, such as perspective and realism, first developed during the Renaissance in the 1400s.

neo-Expressionism: A style of modern painting where the human body is recognizable but portrayed in a violent, emotional way with vivid, garish colors.

realism: In art, a method of depicting subjects in a lifelike, realistic manner without idealizing or embellishing the image.

saltimbanques: Street acrobats and traveling circus artists, often subjects in French poems and paintings, depicted as symbols of misery and social alienation. Picasso depicted *saltimbanques* in a more positive light.

For Further Reading

Books

Linda Bolton, *Surrealists*. Chicago: Heinemann Library, 2003. Discusses the characteristics of the surrealism movement which began in Paris in 1924 and presents biographies of twelve surrealist artists.

Valeriano Bozal et al., *Picasso, from Caricature to Metamorphosis of Style*. Burlington, VT: Lund Humphries, 2003. This book accompanies a major exhibition at the Museu Picasso, Barcelona, and is the first to examine the distortion of the figure as a central creative force in Picasso's art. Caricatures, monsters, puppets, and grotesque figures populate the pages of this book, which is illustrated with over four hundred reproductions of Picasso's paintings, drawings, sculptures, ceramics, and prints.

Rosie Dickins, *The Usborne Introduction to Art: In Association with the National Gallery, London*. Tulsa, OK: EDC, 2004. Detailed introduction to the history of art. The text includes Internet links about featured artists along with examples of their work and works by related artists. Covers the Renaissance, modern art, and more.

Jaime Sabartés, *Picasso: An Intimate Portrait*. New York: Prentice, 1948. A book written by a close friend with chapters about Picasso's early life, first years in Paris, and the late 1930s when he was a widely recognized success.

Jeremy Wallis, *Cubists*. Chicago: Heinemann Library, 2003. Discusses the characteristics of the cubism movement, which began in the first decade of the twentieth century, and presents biographies of thirteen cubist artists including Georges Braque, Juan Gris, and Pablo Picasso.

Jeffrey S. Weiss, *Picasso: The Cubist Portraits of Fernande Olivier*. Washington, DC: National Gallery of Art, 2003. From an exhibition held at the National Gallery of Art, featuring more than sixty portraits Picasso executed of his companion Fernande Olivier between spring and winter 1909. These works reveal a level of experimentation that stands out in the history of portraiture and coincides with the invention of cubism.

Web Sites

Museu Picasso (www.museupicasso.bcn.es/eng/index_eng.htm). The official Web site of the Picasso Museum in Barcelona, Spain, featuring a detailed biography of the painter paired with examples of his work from every period of his lifework.

Pablo Picasso: Official Web Site (www.picasso.fr/anglais/index.htm). The authorized site for Picasso with articles about his work, his family tree, exhibitions, and examples of his art.

Pablo Picasso's *The Tragedy*, National Gallery of Art (www.nga.gov/feature/picasso/index.shtm). A fascinating exhibit that shows the metamorphosis of several of Picasso's paintings, including *The Tragedy*, through the use of infrared reflectography, a process that allows a special camera to penetrate varnish and paint layers, revealing underdrawing or compositional changes beneath the final paint layer.

Index

About the Author

Stuart A. Kallen is the prolific author of more than two hundred fifty nonfiction books for children and young adults. He has written on topics ranging from the theory of relativity to the history of world music. In addition, Kallen has written award-winning children's videos and television scripts. In his spare time, Kallen is a singer/songwriter/guitarist in San Diego, California.